THE
SEVEN
SPIRITS *of* GOD

EXPERIENCING
THRONE ROOM REALITIES

CHRIS REED

FOREWORD BY RICK JOYNER

MorningStar Publications
www.MorningStarMinistries.org

The Seven Spirits of God
By Chris Reed

**Distributed by MorningStar Publications, Inc.,
a division of MorningStar Fellowship Church
375 Star Light Drive, Fort Mill, SC 29715**

**www.MorningStarMinistries.org
1-800-542-0278**

ISBN: 978-1-60708-706-9

For a free catalog of MorningStar resources, please call 1-800-542-0278

ENDORSEMENTS

I'm reading Chris Reed's first book, The Seven Spirits of God, *and am already sharing what I'm discovering with others. Chris is a profoundly gifted prophet whose voice is greatly needed in an hour when Ahabs and Jezebels and Elijahs must inevitably collide.*

—Dr. Lance Wallnau, CEO of Lance Learning Group

As we move closer to the end of this age and the beginning of the kingdom age, we will understand more and more about throne room activity and worship. Clearly the seven lamps of fire burning before the throne are of paramount importance. It is now a present-day mandate to understand the functioning of the seven Spirits of God and how the sons of the kingdom will carry such a great responsibility. Chris' book The Seven Spirits of God *is a blueprint to help us understand this amazing biblical reality. Not only does Chris address the function of each of these spiritual endowments, but also the throne room activity surrounding the Lord's throne and the manifestation of His kingdom power. We must be carriers of the Lord's Spirit in fullness to achieve our great mandate for the harvest. I believe each reader will be blessed by this book and the impartation it conveys.*

—Paul Keith Davis, Founder of WhiteDove Ministries

One of my favorite 'younger' prophets is Chris Reed. Chris is very mature in his understanding of the Word. He displays that understanding in his new book, The Seven Spirits of God: Experiencing Throne Room Realities. *Just as these seven aspects and expressions of the one Holy Spirit occurred in the early church, they will occur again in the present-day and latter-day church. Therefore, this book is a must to understand our corporate identity as the Holy Spirit manifests these realities of Himself in us. The church today rarely experiences the Holy Spirit in all His fullness.* The Seven Spirits of God *will not only help you pray but is also a sign of what we are watching for. This book represents how the Lord taught His disciples to pray…'on earth as it is in heaven.'*

—Chuck D. Pierce, President of Glory of Zion International at Global Spheres Center

I am honored and privileged to write a full, wholehearted endorsement for Chris Reed's awesome new book of revelations concerning the seven Spirits of God. Without question, Chris Reed has a powerful and productive prophetic anointing. The body of Christ will be greatly blessed by his powerful book revealing The Seven Spirits of God. *You will be greatly blessed and encouraged as you drink in the awesome revelations to dig deeper into these powerful revelations and insights. Truly you will be blessed and enriched by the study of this important book to aid in understanding more concerning the manifestation of God's glory.*

—Bobby Conner, Founder of Eagles View Ministries

Chris Reed's book The Seven Spirits of God *sets a new bench-mark in our understanding of the working of the Holy Spirit. Without deconstructing the unity of the Holy Spirit, Chris describes the sevenfold Spirit of God described in Isaiah 11:2 and how each dimension of the Spirit affects our ability to walk with and serve the Lord. I heartily endorse this book for all who seek to walk in clarity, power, and spiritual maturity.*

—Ken Fish, Founder of Orbis Ministries

DEDICATION

I would like to dedicate this book to my family:

To my parents, Lee and Donna Reed, for leading me to
Christ and to the power of the Holy Spirit.

To my wife, Missy, for always supporting my calling
and ministry and walking with me through the ups
and downs of life and ministry.

To my children CJ, Madison, Athena, Hutton,
Ben, and Ellie. You are my inheritance, and I pray
that I will impart to you a deep spiritual reality for
your own lives and a true spiritual hunger.

Also, thanks to Dan Reise for introducing me to
the greater prophetic community and to the great
spiritual heritage he possesses.

To Dr. Mark Hanby, a spiritual father to many,
and a man who was patient with me and helped me
in major crossroads of my life.

And to Rick Joyner for choosing to invest in me,
for inviting me to become part of the great ministry
at MorningStar, and for the privilege
of becoming your successor.

TABLE of CONTENTS

FOREWORD

By Rick Joyner

Chris Reed's book *The Seven Spirits of God* is more than an interesting and remarkable book. Typical of Chris' teachings, he takes this unfathomable subject and explains it with such clarity and insight that it is not only deeply moored to Scripture, but it is also living, practical truth filled with illumination on the Spirit and nature of God.

I John 4:8 says, **"He who does not love does not know God, for God is love."** This means many things, but most importantly, it means it is not possible to know God without loving Him, nor is it possible to love Him without knowing Him.

Since loving God is the "greatest commandment" and our number one purpose as human beings, we will be successful in this life to the degree that we love Him. Thus, knowledge about Him that would compel us to love Him more is the most important knowledge we can have. The knowledge contained in this book can help us know Him better.

We may *think* we have eternal life if we believe in Jesus and His atonement. These are necessary, but such faith cannot be possible without knowing Him. The better we know Him, the more we will believe in Him. When Jesus prayed to the Father in John 17:3, He declared, **"This is eternal life, that they may know You, the only true God, and Jesus Christ whom You have sent."**

There is much more to faith than just knowing who He is. Demons know who He is and are not saved. The Greek word translated "know" in this text implies a deep, personal relationship, like husbands and wives know each other. The longer they live together, the more they learn about each other, including things perhaps no one else knows.

We may think the Scriptures that reveal things about God, like the ones in this book, are some kind of mysterious knowledge meant only for the most mature, super-spiritual saints. On the contrary, this is basic knowledge *every* believer should know. If this book helps us to know Him better, it will help us love Him more, and loving God is the most important requirement of this life.

To live with a devotion to loving God as our highest priority is to live by the highest wisdom we can have. How would you like to live a life in which failure is not possible? Yet the Bible says, **"Love never fails" (see I Corinthians 13:8)**. Since loving God is the highest kind of love, a life of loving Him above all others is the most successful life we can live.

As our friend Peter Lord often said, "The main thing is to keep the main thing the main thing." When he first said this to me, we were having lunch. I resolved then to make that the main compass by which I would live my life. I do not presume to have done this perfectly, but I cannot imagine life without this.

The "main thing" is loving God, and we cannot love His people, other people, our calling, our country, or anything else if we do not love God above all others. To do this is to live the greatest life we can live on this earth and is the best preparation for eternity.

I have spent most of my more than fifty years as a Christian in ministry. I have loved it and cannot imagine a better, more wonderful, fulfilling life. I have spoken at conferences all over the world and shared the speaking with some of the best preachers, teachers, and ministers of our time, and perhaps of all time. I would not trade this experience for any other. However, it is a true statement that more than ninety percent of all Christian preaching and teaching today is about us and not God.

These messages about who we are, what we are called to do, how to be overcomers, and how to live breakthrough lives are all great, and I am thankful for them. Nevertheless, I do not believe we will become who we are called to be, do what we are called to do, overcome as we should, or experience the transcendent life of true Christianity by looking at ourselves. The apostolic message in the first century was, **"They preached Christ, and the resurrection from the dead" (see Acts 4:2, 17:18).**

That seemed to work well for them. The New Testament letters written by the apostles have much to say about us. However, we will not be or do what are called to be and do simply by looking at ourselves. Instead, we must see and be changed by His glory (see II Corinthians 3:18).

I am so thankful Chris' first book is about God and not just us. I believe he is one of a new breed of ministers God is raising up to recover the apostolic gospel to preach Christ and the resurrection. When this happens, I believe we will see much more of Christ in His people, and we will walk in the strength and authority to which we are called.

Still, I love the messages that exhort and encourage us to be what we are called to be and to live in the victory for which Jesus paid the ultimate price. These are important truths, but "the main thing is to keep the main thing the main thing." Knowing God and loving Him is the main thing, and everything else that is worthy will come from this—living the highest wisdom, knowing and loving God above all others, and seeking His glory rather than our own.

"Till we all come into the
unity of the faith,
and of the knowledge of
the Son of God,
to a perfect man,
to the measure of the stature
of the fullness of Christ."

(Ephesians 4:13 NKJV)

CHAPTER 1

An Overview of the Seven Spirits

The seven Spirits of God will become more and more relevant as the church comes into its full maturity as an expression of the Son of God and its partnership with the fullness of the Holy Spirit in these last days. We are living in a day when the sons of God and the sons of the wicked one (the wheat and tares) are both coming to full maturity. That is why, now more than ever, we see such clear contrast in our culture between right and wrong, black and white, and truth and error. Never has there been a clearer division between two opposing worldviews, and never has it been more important to capture this revelation of the seven Spirits of God throughout the Bible.

We must learn to express and manifest the fullness of the Holy Spirit, not just individual giftings. I Corinthians 12 declares that there is one Spirit of God but various administrations and giftings. However, when we come together as the body of Christ, we come into His fullness and maturity.

Ephesians 4 reveals that the fivefold ministry—apostle, prophet, evangelist, pastor, and teacher—was given for the edification and maturing of the body to place, train, and equip the saints to do their ministry *until* we come to full maturity as a perfect man. Not perfect men and women (plural) but a perfect man (singular). When the church comes together, our gifts, talents, abilities, and callings mesh so well that we are seen as one entity by God and others. We *are* the body of Christ on earth. That is what the Lord is doing in this hour.

Isaiah 60 speaks of a time when the glory of the Lord will rise on God's people. At the same time, gross darkness will cover the earth and its people. However, when the glory of the Lord rises on God's people, we will come into our full purpose, manifesting Christ to the world in His complete nature and power.

Today, we are living in Romans 8. We are witnessing unique weather patterns and natural disasters. All of creation is groaning through tornadoes, earthquakes, and hurricanes as nature itself groans and waits with birth pangs *until* now for the manifestation of the sons of God (see Romans 8:18-22). Or as Ephesians 4 says, **"till we all come into the unity of the faith, and of the knowledge of the Son of God, to a perfect man, to the measure of the stature of the fullness of Christ"** **(Ephesians 4:13).** Both Ephesians 4 and Romans 8 use the word *till* or *until*. A "till" process is taking place in which we are all waiting for the full expression and manifestation of the sons of God when the church will model Jesus everywhere.

In Paul's letter to the Galatians, he prayed for a "rebirthing" of those who had already been born again. He wrote, **"My little children, of whom I travail in birth again until Christ is formed in you" (Galatians 4:19 KJV).** There's that word "until" again. Those who have been born again can be born into a new, higher level of maturity and power. Acts 10 reveals how Jesus, the firstborn of the new creation, was first to become what we will become when this "rebirthing" takes place: **"How God anointed Jesus of Nazareth with the Holy Spirit and with power, who went about doing good and healing all who were oppressed by the devil"** (see Acts 10:38). This speaks of Christ's nature, the fruit of the Spirit and of healing and deliverance for all who are oppressed by the devil. That is the complete power of God. Jesus was entrusted as a man with power to destroy the works of the devil—sin, sickness, disease, and demonic oppression. He was entrusted as a man with that power because He was fully surrendered and yielded to His Father's will above His natural inclinations.

Soon we, too, will fully express the manifestation of the sons of God with the nature and power of Jesus Christ in the greater works which He promised we would do. Just as He went about doing good and healing, we will have the power to heal, deliver, and do the greater works. Even today, the level of power and authority we are entrusted with is commensurate with the level of the fruit of the Spirit and nature of Christ we have allowed to develop within us. The gifts and fruit of the Spirit are nine each—nine fruit (singular) and nine gifts (plural). The nine gifts are balanced by the nine fruit.

What good is the gift of miracles without the fruit of meekness? No doubt we would start taking credit for those miracles as if we were specially gifted. We are not and should not. The base fruit of the fruit of the Spirit is love, from which all the other fruit flow, but the nine gifts are also given by the nine fruit of the Spirit which also must be developed and grown.

Thus, the body of Christ is at a tipping point. We must decide whether we will be content with the status quo church as we have known it from our denominational backgrounds or seek the fullness of the Spirit and nature of Jesus. Jesus said He would send the Holy Spirit, so we could learn more by the indwelled Spirit than we did when He was here. He said there were yet many things He needed to tell us, but when the Spirit of Truth came, He would teach us all things and remind us of everything Jesus taught us when He was here. In other words, we would know Christ and His ways better by the Spirit than even when He was with us.

That is what the Lord wants to develop through the seven Spirits. He wants us learning, ministering, and teaching by the Spirit in fulfillment of the prophecy in which everyone will know the Lord, no man will teach his neighbor, and no one will need to be taught (see Hebrews 8:11; I John 2:27). We will know more by the Spirit than we could ever ascertain through our reading or intellect. We will process information about Jesus because we know Him by the Spirit—the preferred and advanced way of knowing Him.

People often say, "I wish I could have lived in the time of Jesus and seen His miracles, death, burial, and resurrection." Yet Jesus said those who live in the church age would have a clear advantage over those who were with Him in His earthly ministry. He said we would know when the Spirit of Truth came because He would teach us all things and have a new maturity in the Lord. Growth is something we will see unfold when we walk in the full force of the Holy Spirit.

Would you prefer to live in the time of Jesus and see His miracles and know and touch and hear Him, or know Him by the Spirit, which Jesus said would be better? For those who would still prefer to see Him in His earthly ministry, what is coming will be so much better than even in those days! The beauty of the body of Christ walking in the fullness of the Spirit will not be limited to one Jesus walking on earth, but will include many expressions of Jesus walking on earth through God's sons and daughters.

Those who walk in the fullness of Christ's power and authority will dethrone demons, principalities, powers, and governing spirits over regions which are now influencing all the evil and craziness we are witnessing on earth. This is being directly influenced by principalities and powers enthroned and entrenched in those geographical regions. We will replace those spirits with God's authority and kingdom on earth. What an exciting time this is!

The seven Spirits of God is a complete number. The Lord created the heavens and the earth in six days and rested on the seventh day. Since then, the number seven has been biblically associated with completion and perfection. If you hunger for the deep things of God, if your heart longs for Him, the Holy Spirit wants to reveal the fullness of Christ to you through a revelation of the Spirit of wisdom and understanding, the Spirit of counsel and might, and the Spirit of knowledge and the fear of the Lord.

God is searching throughout the earth for those who desire to go beyond the come-and-go gifts of the Spirit—people who want to advance to a place where the sevenfold Holy Spirit becomes an abiding, flowing river of God's presence who is constant, continual, available, and present when we need

Him. When the seven Spirits of God come to fullness in us, we will fully reflect Christ's nature and power.

In Revelation 1:4, we find the seven Spirits of God: **"John, to the seven churches which are in Asia: Grace to you and peace from Him who is and who was and who is to come, and from the seven Spirits who are before His throne."** Then in Revelation 3:1: **"And to the angel of the church in Sardis write, 'These things says He who has the seven Spirits of God and the seven stars: I know your works, that you have a name that you are alive, but you are dead.'"**

Also, in Revelation 4:5: **"And from the throne preceded lightnings, thunderings, and voices. Seven lamps of fire were burning before the throne, which are the seven Spirits of God."** And finally, in Revelation 5:6: **"And I looked, and behold, in the midst of the throne and of the four living creatures, and in the midst of the elders, stood a Lamb as though it had been slain, having seven horns and seven eyes, which are the seven Spirits of God sent out into all the earth."**

The seven Spirits of God are mentioned several times when John is caught up into the heavens and experiences the apocalypse or unveiling revelation of Jesus Christ. Repeatedly, when Jesus corresponds with His church or speaks of His power or message, the seven Spirits come up, encoded in Revelation. However, unlike Revelation, which only *mentions* the seven Spirits of God, there is one place in the Bible that *names* the seven Spirits of God: Isaiah 11:2.

Isaiah 11 speaks of the future Messiah who, of course, is the Lord Jesus Christ. Isaiah declares that the seven Spirits of

God will rest on Jesus, the Messiah. Here is what he wrote: **"The Spirit of the Lord shall rest upon Him, the Spirit of wisdom and understanding, the Spirit of counsel and might, the Spirit of knowledge and of the fear of the Lord" (Isaiah 11:2).**

Now these are not seven *separate* Spirits but rather seven *expressions* or manifestations of the Holy Spirit, or the seven-fold Holy Spirit:

1. The Spirit of the Lord.
2. The Spirit of wisdom.
3. The Spirit of understanding (or revelation).
4. The Spirit of counsel.
5. The Spirit of might (signs, wonders, and miracles).
6. The Spirit of knowledge.
7. The Spirit of the fear of the Lord.

These are seven aspects or expressions of the one Holy Spirit. In fact, the Classic Edition of the Amplified Bible uses the term **"[the sevenfold Holy Spirit]"** in brackets in Revelation 1:4. The Holy Spirit is not split; He will simply manifest wisdom when we need it. When we walk in the fullness of the Holy Spirit and have need of the Spirit of knowledge, or the Spirit of counsel and might, they will be manifested to us. The mystery of the seven Spirits of God is this: they are distinct but one. They are seven functions, expressions, or manifestations of the Holy Spirit.

However, to understand more about the nature of the Holy Spirit, we must have a separate definition for each of the seven Spirits. By naming and defining the seven Spirits, we can learn much more about the fullness of the Holy Spirit.

Then the fullness of the Spirit will become more than some vague concept without goal, definition, or insight.

When John writes to the churches in Revelation about the seven Spirits of God, it's interesting that he also writes about seven messengers and seven churches—three sets of seven. These seven churches were clearly not the only churches in the world at the time but were seven "handpicked" churches from Asia Minor, which may represent seven churches from any given point in church history. We can certainly see the descriptions of the seven churches reflected in the modern church and perhaps the Western Church most consistently.

For example, the Laodicean church, the seventh church, is described as having an abundance of materialism but being lukewarm spiritually. Jesus seemed to reserve the greatest rebuke for this church. Of course, not all churches today, even in the West, fit this description. Jesus is simply addressing what was predominant at the time. Some churches were more faithful, like the church of Philadelphia. Even today, certain churches and ministries stand out uniquely among the churches of the nations. The Lord highlights these to the greater body of Christ for special purposes because they do not succumb to the Laodicean spirit of lethargy and apathy of our time, which is often exacerbated by abundant possessions, materialism, and freedom.

Some see these seven messengers in Revelation, which are also called "angels," as lead pastors or senior leaders of the seven churches. Others see the seven messengers as seven angels representing seven individuals who, at various times throughout church history, became predominant leaders.

I believe there is truth in both these views. I also believe the Laodicean spirit is dominant in the Western Church right now.

That does *not* mean we, as individuals or churches, must acquiesce to that. We can rise above and challenge that spirit saying, "No, Jesus called us to be overcomers." The entire goal of Revelation is for us to become overcomers, but to be that, we each must overcome our unique challenges, struggles, and propensities in our own flesh and minds which qualify us to become part of that company of overcomers.

In Scripture, there are different Hebrew and Greek words that are translated "angel." For example, in Haggai 1:13, Haggai, a human being, is called "the Lord's messenger" or "angel." Here, the Hebrew word *malak* is used, which means "messenger" or "angel." Of course, the theophany or prein-carnate Christ in Genesis 16:7-13 and throughout the Old Testament is also often called "the angel of the Lord." This could also be true of the seven angels, messengers, churches, and even the seven Spirits of God in Revelation.

I remind you that Revelation is primarily a book about Jesus Christ, not about an antichrist. In fact, John called it, "The Revelation of Jesus Christ." It is about knowing and seeing Him by the Spirit, so that any veils in our souls which may hinder us from seeing spiritually may be removed, and our spiritual eyes may be opened to see and behold Him as He is. In other words, seeing Christ for who He is—not who the church, religion, or theologians tell us He is—will bring trans-formation in us. Beholding and knowing Christ for ourselves, as He reveals Himself to us, will change us.

Before we explore each of the seven Spirits, understand that, just as the preincarnate Christ of the Old Testament is described as "the angel of the Lord," these seven "angels" in Revelation can also mean seven Holy Spirit expressions. Since we cannot see a spirit, the Holy Spirit can come to us in angelic forms, meaning visibly and tangibly. So, the seven Spirits could be seen or described as an angel of the fear of the Lord, an angel of the Spirit of counsel and might, or an angel of the Spirit of wisdom—as visible, manifest expressions of the sevenfold Holy Spirit.

Just as Christ was revealed in the Old Testament in the form of an angel, the sevenfold Holy Spirit can be uniquely revealed as seven expressions of the Holy Spirit in the form of angels. Each of the seven Spirits of God can represent a personality or function of the Holy Spirit. Thus, it would be proper to say, "the Spirit of wisdom *is* the Holy Spirit." There is a personality in the Spirit of wisdom that we do not find elsewhere, and to know the Spirit of wisdom is to know a portion of the Holy Spirit.

I had an encounter a few years ago about the seven Spirits of God. I was caught up in the Spirit and met the angel called, "The fear of the Lord." He had a blue sash and a glowing expression, and I felt a sensation of trembling. In this experience, he invited me to walk through a door. Understandably trembling, in shock, and with trepidation because of the sense of holiness and reverence I felt, I walked through the door at his invitation. I saw a large library in heaven. The room contained many scrolls of destiny, history, and accounts of what had happened through eternity past in the realm of the Spirit and the realm of the earth.

He invited me to an old section of the library. Over it was written, "The Supernatural Section." When I looked in this section, I was drawn to one book. I saw the title on the spine of the book. It read, *The Seven Spirits of God*. There were many other books there, but this one was highlighted to me and seemed to be the only one that appealed to me at that moment. I grabbed it and saw the words, *The Spirit of the Lord* on the front cover.

Then I opened the front cover and found five thick white pages. Each page was as thick as a book, and each page had a name written on it. I turned to the first page, it read "The Spirit of Wisdom," the second page, "The Spirit of Understanding or Revelation," the third page, "The Spirit of Counsel," the fourth page, "The Spirit of Might," and the fifth and last page, "The Spirit of Knowledge." Then I flipped over to the back cover and written on it was, "The Spirit of the Fear of the Lord."

As I held the book, I was overcome by all the colors, lights, and euphoric feelings of joy and peace, yet also reverence and awe. I glanced up for a second, then looked back down at the back cover, and the words, "The Spirit of the Fear of the Lord" had been ripped off and were lying on top of the five pages and front cover. Then I took the back cover, pulled it away, and the five pages in the middle fell to the floor. So, in my right hand, I was holding the back cover which had read, "The Spirit of the Fear of the Lord," and in my left I was holding the front cover which read, "The Spirit of the Lord."

Then the angel, who was now standing behind me, asked if I understood what was being revealed to me through this encounter. He said, "When the fear of the Lord is taken away from the church, the supernatural acts of the Holy Spirit are lost as well. The pages fall out." He said, "Notice that what you are holding in your left hand was the front cover which read, 'The Spirit of the Lord.'" He said, "When the fear of the Lord is taken out, the supernatural elements of the Holy Spirit are lost." He said, "All you were left holding was the atmosphere or presence of the Lord."

When the angel said this, I knew what he meant. He did not mean the Spirit of the Lord was lacking in or of Himself, but as we often hear in many contemporary Spirit-filled church services, "We feel the Spirit of the Lord here," or "We feel the presence of the Lord in this place." Yet how many leave not having been healed by the Spirit of might? How many leave not having their sicknesses or troubles thwarted by the Spirit of counsel? How many leave with questions and uncertainties about life having never experienced the Spirit of wisdom? Most people's experience with the Pentecostal and Charismatic worlds consists of a feeling or atmosphere with little display of God's supernatural power. That is what the angel meant would be lost when the fear of the Lord is taken away.

I believe much of this has come from the abuses of hyper-grace teaching, which has largely removed the reverence of the Lord. I believe with all my heart we can be big believers in grace theology and still have reverence for the Lord. However, some individuals have taken grace to such an extreme that people have become careless and flippant about holy or supernatural things.

The Holy Spirit is a gentleman. He is described as "a dove." A dove can become frightened. The Holy Spirit is never frightened, but His nature is gentle, and He loves to be welcomed. So, in the Holy Spirit we see a dove, in Christ we see a lamb, and in the Father, we see a lion. Christ has the dual nature of a lion and a lamb. His first coming was as a lamb; His second coming will be as the lion of the tribe of Judah. Now He is with us in the form of the Holy Spirit. "On the wings of a snow white dove," He has come. The more we mature in the things of God spiritually, mentally, and emotionally, the more the Holy Spirit will reveal Christ in, to, and through us, and the less our old nature will be seen.

The seven Spirits of God are also depicted in Scripture as seven lampstands or as the seven golden candlesticks of the menorah. Again, Revelation 4:5 says, **"from the throne proceeded lightnings, thunderings, and voices. Seven lamps of fire were burning before the throne, which are the seven Spirits of God."** The seven golden candlesticks or lampstands burn before the throne in heaven, which represent the presence and glory of God. The menorah or lampstand was found in the Holy Place, the second dimension of Moses' tabernacle. It is a prophetic representation of the Holy Spirit or sevenfold Holy Spirit.

The menorah, or seven golden candlesticks, was just in front of the ark of the covenant in the Holy of Holies, which prophetically represented the throne of God. That is why there was a mercy seat with cherubim hovering over the mercy seat. Just as the ark of the covenant was an earthly representation of God's throne, the seven golden candlesticks were an earthly representation of the sevenfold Holy Spirit. Likewise, in Revelation, the seven Spirits of God (the menorah) were right before the throne of God (the ark of the covenant).

Moses built the tabernacle according to the heavenly pattern God showed him on the mount when he was visiting with the Lord. Likewise, in Revelation 4, when John was in the throne room of God, he saw the seven lamps of fire burning before the throne of God. It is an exact picture of the tabernacle, the Holy Place, the Holy of Holies, and a symbolic representation of the seven Spirits of God.

God has also revealed the seven Spirits of God in the form of eyes. Again, Revelation 5:6: **"And I looked, and behold, in the midst of the throne and of the four living creatures, and in the midst of the elders, stood a Lamb as though it had been slain, having seven horns and seven eyes, which are the seven Spirits of God sent out into all the earth."** Revelation 4:8 tells us the four living creatures which stood before God's throne each had six wings full of eyes around and within. Every time "eyes" are mentioned in Scripture they refer to the omniscience of God—the all-seeing, all-knowing omniscient nature of God and His Holy Spirit.

II Chronicles 16:9 says, **"For the eyes of the Lord run to and fro throughout the whole earth, to show Himself strong on behalf of those whose heart is loyal to Him."** Also, Jesus quoted Isaiah 11:1 in reference to Himself, which says, **"There shall come forth a Rod from the stem of Jesse, and a Branch shall grow out of his roots."** So, Jesus is also compared to a branch.

This is significant because Zechariah prophesies about this "branch" in relation to the seven Spirits: **"Hear, O Joshua, the high priest, you and your companions who sit before you, for they are a wondrous sign; for behold, I am bringing forth My Servant the BRANCH. For behold, the stone**

that I have laid before Joshua; upon the stone are seven eyes." (see Zechariah 3:8-9).

Here, in Zechariah, we see the sign of God's servant, the Branch, and the stone which has seven eyes. In Isaiah 11:1, we see Jesus, who would come as a Rod from the stem of Jesse and a Branch that would grow out of his roots. Then in Revelation 5:6, we see on Jesus, the Lamb that was slain, seven horns and seven eyes, which are the seven Spirits of God sent out into all the earth.

Isaiah 11:1 talks about the Branch, and Isaiah 11:2 talks about the Spirit of the Lord which shall rest upon Him, the seven Spirits of God. When we connect all these prophecies together, we see Jesus is fully expressed by the sevenfold Spirit of God with seven eyes and seven horns. Horns are prophetically symbolic of complete power. That is why Zechariah went on to say, **"Not by might nor by power, but by My Spirit, says the Lord of hosts" (see Zechariah 4:6).**

Lastly, Zechariah 4:10 says, **"For who has despised the day of small things? For these seven rejoice to see the plumb line in the hand of Zerubbabel."** What "seven"? **"They are the eyes of the Lord that go to and fro throughout the whole earth."** They are the seven Spirits of God which make Him the omniscient, all-knowing, all-seeing God.

This ought to excite us when we are reminded of Psalm 32:8, where He promises in His Word, **"I will instruct you and teach you in the way you should go; I will guide you with My eye."** I am reminded of the chorus of the old hymn, "By and by, when the morning comes, when the saints of God are gathered home, we will tell the story how we've overcome; we will understand it better by and by." Verse one says, "But He'll guide us with His eye, and we'll follow till we die; we will understand it better by and by."

The eye of the Lord is connected to the Spirit of the Lord, and His eye is on us just as His eye is on the sparrow. His Spirit is on us, and through His eye we can see clearly. From His eye and Spirit, He looks and searches us within and without. Those seven eyes and seven Spirits feel at home in us. We can also see with His eyes, which makes the prophetic so real— seeing and foreseeing future events, circumstances, the true nature of a matter, and the secrets of the heart. The more we are aware of the Spirit, the more we will have His nature, fruit, and power.

Those seven eyes can become the eyes through which we see. We want to see as Jesus sees. We want to be like the four living creatures in Revelation, which had eyes around and within. This means they could look within themselves intro-spectively to make sure their hearts and motives were right, while simultaneously seeing everything happening around them. The sevenfold Holy Spirit will enable you to do this. He will give you discernment in front and behind you, to where you literally have eyes behind your head, just like these four living creatures. Talk about having a prophetic perspective of yourself and others!

The golden lampstand represents the sevenfold Holy Spirit, just as the seven eyes and seven horns represent the sevenfold Holy Spirit's vision and power. The menorah has seven can-dlesticks, or branches, which all run through the middle staff, or pillar. The middle staff has one candleholder at the top and three branches running through it. This also gives meaning to the scriptural promise and prophecy of Jesus as our "bridge" or mediator (see I Timothy 2:5). The three branches or sticks of the menorah are bent in perfect formation forming seven lights at the top.

All this correlates to the sevenfold Holy Spirit in Isaiah 11:2. On the menorah, there is one lampstand by itself in the middle, then three couplings and three branches each containing two lampstands. Likewise, in Isaiah 11:2: **"The Spirit**

of the Lord shall rest upon Him, the Spirit of wisdom and understanding, the Spirit of counsel and might, the Spirit of knowledge and of the fear of the Lord." The same three couplings in the menorah are in Isaiah 11:2. The Spirit of the Lord stands by itself; the other six are coupled together. Thus, if you have the Spirit of counsel, it is usually followed by the Spirit of might.

For example, if the Lord shows you by the Spirit of counsel that someone has cancer, you can expect the Spirit of might to show up to heal them. The same is true with the Spirit of wisdom and understanding or revelation. What good is revelation without wisdom to implement it? How would you know when or even if to share it? If someone has a great revelation gift or the ability to unfold Bible mysteries, they usually have great wisdom to explain it.

The same is true with the Spirit of knowledge and the fear of the Lord. Those who have a strong anointing for true biblical knowledge, the ways of God, and the innerworkings of the universe, typically have the fear of the Lord coupled with that knowledge. With great revelation knowledge often comes the fear of the Lord to balance it out, such as when Paul received his thorn in the flesh, lest he become exalted above measure by the abundance of revelations (see II Corinthians 12:7). We need the sevenfold Holy Spirit now more than ever, and I am excited to learn and to share the rest of the sevenfold Holy Spirit with you.

CHAPTER 2

The Spirit of the Lord

Now that we have been introduced to the seven Spirits of God and have a scriptural foundation for the sevenfold Holy Spirit, let's examine more closely the first of the seven Spirits mentioned in Isaiah 11:2, the Spirit of the Lord.

First, we need to understand there is a distinct difference between the nine gifts of the Spirit in I Corinthians 12:7-10 and the seven mantles of the Holy Spirit or sevenfold Holy Spirit in Isaiah 11:2. The nine gifts of the Spirit are a word of knowledge, a word of wisdom, gifts of healings, gift of faith, working of miracles, discerning of spirits, gift of prophecy, gift of tongues, and gift of interpretation of tongues. The seven mantles, or sevenfold Holy Spirit, are the Spirit of the Lord, Spirit of wisdom, Spirit of understanding (or revelation), Spirit of counsel, Spirit of might, Spirit of knowledge, and Spirit of the fear of the Lord.

These seven mantles of the Holy Spirit are the seven Spirits of God which descended and rested on Jesus like a dove at His baptism. We could also say it this way: The seven Spirits of God operating in our lives are the nine gifts of the Spirit in their full maturity. For example, Jesus did not simply operate in a word of knowledge as one of the nine gifts of the Spirit. Instead, He operated in the Spirit of knowledge as an endless access point. Again, Jesus did not simply operate in the gifts of healings but in the Spirit of might. This mantle did not lift from Him but rather remained upon Him after His baptism.

Now the Spirit of the Lord distributes to each one gifts of the Spirit as He sees fit (see I Corinthians 12:11). This means they come and go. For example, if you are given gifts of healings, you may pray for ten people, but only seven of the ten may receive healing. Though it is God's will to heal them all, and though Jesus healed them all, why were three not healed? Or why were three healed and seven not? These are all mysteries we do not fully understand.

Some blame this on a lack of faith in the person who is sick. Others blame it on a lack of faith in the person praying for the sick. Neither may be totally right. Rather the frequency and consistency may be the difference between the nine gifts of the Spirit and the seven Spirits of God.

I have found in my own ministry there are times when it seems like the heavens are open and I could know every secret of the heart that is laid bare before me in that room. Yet there are other times when I only receive small bits of revelation. The latter seems to happen more consistently. No one likes to be put on the spot, but occasionally someone will come up to me and say, "Do you have something from the Lord for me?" Often I can receive something accurate for them simply by drawing on that more consistent level of gifting. But then that gifting will increase substantially after I have preached the Word and then operated in ministry.

This is the Lord confirming His Word with signs following, just as He confirmed the apostles' words with signs and wonders (see Mark 16:20; Acts 2:42-43). When the Word is preached, the Spirit will confirm it, because the Word and the Spirit agree. That is why we must worship Him in spirit and in truth.

Then there are those times when we can have access to an endless supply of the Spirit of counsel and might and can tell a hundred people their physical conditions and see every one of them healed. Few through history operated on such a level of consistent demonstration. They operated in more than just the gift of a word of knowledge or gifts of healings. We know this because their success and consistency were substantially higher than most in the body of Christ. The difference in Jesus' ministry was that the Spirit of the Lord rested on Him after His baptism.

There is also a difference between being born of the Spirit and being baptized or filled with the Spirit. Every person who truly repents of their sins and confesses faith in the Lord Jesus will experience a change inside them. We hear stories how people prayed a prayer and meant it, and everything changed. They were born of the Spirit. Then there's a further experience called being baptized with the Spirit. Not everyone is walking in that. It's a gift, a promise. We see this in Acts. But even beyond being baptized in the Spirit, there is a higher level that comes when the Spirit rests upon us.

Many people experience the comings and goings of the Spirit, but few have the Spirit resting upon them. It's been said, "The Lord has worked through many but rested on few." There is much truth in that statement. Something substantial happened to Jesus. There was a tremendous change in Jesus after He turned thirty and was baptized. The Spirit of the Lord descended upon Him, the heavens were opened, and the voice of the Father spoke when the Spirit descended. From that day forward, there was a consistency and continuity of miracles, signs, and wonders because the Spirit rested upon Him.

Now Jesus was born of the Spirit in a unique way. He was both Almighty God and fully man. Yet the man, Christ Jesus, had the Holy Spirit His whole life, who kept Him from sinning. That is why He lived a perfect life. He was fully God and fully man. We know something changed after His baptism because we don't read about any miracles happening prior to His baptism. And if we are honest, most of the church today is a picture of what Jesus was before His baptism. We have been born of the Spirit; we are justified by faith as though we never sinned. But there is coming a baptism of fire, a baptism of the Spirit resting upon us, which will kick the supernatural into overdrive.

Few in church history have experienced such a baptism, but very soon I believe there will come a corporate baptism that will include a company or remnant of the church. This is the Romans 8 manifestation of the sons of God for which all of creation groans and waits. This is the Galatians 4 prophecy, "till Christ be formed in you." This is the Ephesians 4 prophecy in which the fivefold ministry perfects the saints for the work of the ministry, till we all come into the unity of the faith and of the knowledge of the Son of God, to a perfect man. The word "till" means waiting for something that is yet to happen—a remnant, a company of God's people who will be baptized in the fullness of the Holy Spirit. So far, we have only received the down payment. Soon we will receive the full inheritance of the sevenfold Holy Spirit.

The Apostle Paul said we had received the "earnest," or down payment, of our inheritance (see Ephesians 1:13-14). Still, he, Simon Peter, and John experienced incredible miracles. And still today, I know I have consistently seen supernatural miracles in my own life and ministry.

A recent testimony was shared after I called out a married couple. I heard the song, "Christmas Don't Be Late" by Alvin and the Chipmunks. Then I spoke to the husband and learned his name was Alvin, which I did not know. I told him about some things God was doing. Then I saw in the Spirit his wife had a neurological condition. I told her, "Christmas is coming early! God is healing you today, and if the Lord reveals it, He intends to heal it." Two weeks later, we received a written testimony from Alvin saying his wife did have a neurological condition and had not been able to read for twenty-five years. That day, after that word was given, she was healed and can now read again.

This is just one of many examples of the Spirit of counsel and might, but this is only the tip of the iceberg. We are only scratching the surface on the Spirit of counsel and might. The Lord wants to give all of us more than just the down payment of which Paul spoke more than once. He wants all of us to walk in the fullness of the seven Spirits, and "seven" means complete. He wants all of us to be complete and perfect representatives of Jesus.

After Jesus was baptized in the Jordan River, He accelerated into a new ministry. This last-day ministry will come after a new baptism. Lord, bring on the corporate man, the mature man in Christ, who will bring us to a new level of the supernatural and to a new corporate manifestation of the Son of God like we have never seen before. May we demonstrate the powers of the age to come *before* it comes.

We see many examples of this in Scripture. Jesus demonstrated more than what we would call the nine gifts of the Spirit. Not to diminish spiritual gifts, but they can also come to full maturity just like the fruit of the Spirit can grow, develop, and mature inside every believer.

Imagine how excited Nathanael must have been when he realized heaven was open and no longer shut off to him. Jesus not only *told* Nathanael heaven was open to him but also *proved* heaven was open to him by a word of knowledge. He saw him under the fig tree earlier that day. In essence, Jesus said, "You thought you were alone this morning, but I saw you under the fig tree." Nathanael asked, "Who are You? And how could You know this when no one else was around or saw me?" Surely Nathanael's faith skyrocketed knowing that heaven would be open to him from that moment. God was no longer some distant deity in another galaxy. He could now have access to God through Christ any time.

Nathanael answered and said to Him, "Rabbi, You are the Son of God! You are the King of Israel!"
Jesus answered and said to him, "Because I said to you, 'I saw you under the fig tree,' do you believe? You will see greater things than these."
And He said to him, "Most assuredly, I say to you, hereafter you shall see heaven open, and the angels of God

ascending and descending upon the Son of Man"
(John 1:49-51).

Many people get excited when they hear a word of knowledge. You tell them by revelation about some dream they had, or details about what their doctor said, or you tell them about a spiritual experience they had the night before. They are amazed when they realize you could not have known that except by a word of knowledge.

However, Jesus said to Nathanael, "Don't be impressed by a word of knowledge. That is only your historic faith. Be impressed when the heavens are opened to you, when you can see in the angelic realm, angels ascending and descending. That's when the kingdom of heaven has come to you. You can now experience God in a profound new way. That word of knowledge was only to make you aware that the heavens are open, and the angelic realm is now coming down over your life."

I encourage those of you who have seen real prophetic ministry or have had words of knowledge come to you. This is more than just revealing the secrets of someone's heart, or someone's health condition, or where they live. It's great to know by revelation conversations people had, but the real purpose of a word of knowledge is to bring to the place where we can all say, "Spirit of the Lord, there is an open heaven available to me, and I want to access that whenever I can."

Words of knowledge may introduce you to healing, but it shouldn't stop there. Many do stop there, but what if that is just the gate? What if that is just the beginning or doorway to encountering God all the time? God wants to pull you up the ladder to embrace angels carrying things up and down the ladder, bringing heavenly things to you, and taking your prayers and concerns up the ladder. This is not about a word of knowledge, Nathanael. From now on, you will see angels. You will see heaven open, just as the heavens opened at Jesus' baptism. The voice of God spoke, and the Spirit of God descended and rested upon Him.

I imagine the fresh baptism that is coming on the body of Christ to look like this: going from just being born of the Spirit to a new baptism that takes us to a new level of priestly ministry. With this new baptism, the heavens will be opened to us, God's voice will be renewed in the earth, and the Spirit of the Lord will descend and remain on us. This, to me, is a perfect picture of the seven Spirits of God or sevenfold Holy Spirit.

The Spirit descends, the heavens open, and the voice of God speaks simultaneously across the body of Christ and in all the churches. Then comes a doubling, tripling, and qua-drupling outpouring of the Holy Spirit—open heavens, supernatural signs and wonders, and the voice of God speak-ing clearer than ever. This is what we are heading toward. That is the "till" for which all of creation waits. Next, we will hear a sound from heaven that will release the grace that will super-naturally accelerate us into more than anything the church has ever experienced.

The Lord wants us to operate in this now. He wants us to believe we can hear from Him every day. Today, angelic encounters often happen unaware, but in the days ahead they will become more consistent expressions of the supernatural.

"My heart also instructs me in the night seasons" (see Psalm 16:7). What if the Lord wants to start teaching you every night through dreams, bypassing your conscious mind and going straight to the imagery of your subconscious mind, teaching you everything you need to know about the season ahead? What if the Lord wants to show you in a dream about a place you will be the next day and warn you of a crisis that spares your life and others from disaster? What if the Lord wants to tell you ahead of time about someone who will be your friend and you have already prayed for them? This is not only possible, but also coming.

This is the waiting "till" I keep talking about. **"But as it is written: 'Eye has not seen, nor ear heard, nor have entered into the heart of man the things which God has prepared for those who love Him.' But God has revealed them to us through His Spirit. For the Spirit searches all things, yes, the deep things of God. For what man knows the things of a man except the spirit of the man which is in him? Even so no one knows the things of God except the Spirit of God"** (I Corinthians 2:9-11).

An increase is coming! Eyes cannot describe and ears cannot articulate the things God has prepared for us. We can either forsake them or awaken to them by the Spirit, understanding we have not yet fully walked in them. We have only received the down payment of the Holy Spirit, the earnest of our inheritance, but the fullness is coming.

The Spirit of the Lord is the Holy Spirit in Isaiah 61:1. This is another messianic prophecy, which Jesus quoted and fulfilled in Luke 4:18 when He said, **"The Spirit of the Lord is upon Me, because he has anointed me."** Then Acts 10:38

says, **"How God anointed Jesus of Nazareth with the Holy Spirit and with power, who went about doing good and healing all who were oppressed by the devil, for God was with Him."**

Something profound is coming! If you will only open your heart to it and say, "Lord, I want the fullness of the Holy Spirit. I want to continue to learn, to grow, and to increase the time I spend with You. I want to learn what it means to pray without ceasing. I want to learn what it means to be led by the Spirit." **"For as many as are led by the Spirit of God, they are the sons of God" (see Romans 8:14).** This is the manifestation of the sons of God, which Romans 8 says is coming. All creation is groaning and waiting for this to happen, and the fullness of this is directly tied to us learning to be led by the Spirit.

How much of our lives, every hour of every day, is Spirit led? I admit there are areas in my own life in which I could learn to yield and follow His leading better. One thing we all must learn to master is the grace which has been given to us. Being led by the Spirit is equated with being sons of God.

If you have never been baptized in the Holy Spirit, this is a new covenant experience. We see examples of this beginning in Acts 2:1-4. Then Peter preached, and those who saw the Holy Spirit poured out were pricked in their hearts. They asked, "What shall we do?" Peter said, **"Repent, and let every one of you be baptized in the name of Jesus Christ for the remission of sins; and you shall receive the gift of the Holy Spirit. For the promise is to you and to your children, and to all who are afar off, as many as the Lord our God will call" (see Acts 2:38-39).**

Then we see this manifestation or receiving of the Holy Spirit repeated in Acts 8:16, Acts 10:44-48, and Acts 19:1-6. The most common initial expression of the Holy Spirit is speaking in other tongues, but it is not the only one. Prophesying is another means of initial expression of the Holy Spirit. However, the most common first expression of the indwelling Holy Spirit is the yielding of the tongue to God. It is the unruliest member. God trains our tongue, then tames our spirit man. James 3:8 says, **"no man can tame the tongue."** Yet if a man can have his tongue tamed, he is a perfect and mature man (see James 3:2). This could be why speaking in tongues is the most common initial sign of baptism in the Holy Spirit, but we ought not limit ourselves to that.

If you have never received the Holy Spirit like in the book of Acts, I strongly encourage you to receive Him. Ask the Lord to forgive you. If you have never been water baptized, get water baptized. Then come to the Lord in your time of prayer and expect rivers of living water to flow from your innermost being, bypass your brain, and come out your mouth (see John 7:38-39). Then, as you speak in other tongues and prophesy under the inspiration of the Holy Spirit, remember that a tongue fully yielded and surrendered to the Spirit of the Lord will be the beginning of your maturing into the fullness of the Holy Spirit.

CHAPTER 3

The Spirit of Wisdom

As a church that is advancing in the power and purposes of the Lord, producing a company of overcomers by
the power of the Holy Spirit, and doing the greater works,
one of the greatest revelations we can have is to match this
power with the nature of Jesus. This way, we can operate in
both His nature *and* His power. I Corinthians 2 speaks of a
continuous discovery of God. The more we behold Him, the
more He reveals Himself to us: **"'Eye has not seen, nor ear
heard, nor have entered into the heart of man the things
which God has prepared for those who love Him.' But
God has revealed them to us through His Spirit. For the
Spirit searches, all things, yes, the deep things of God"
(I Corinthians 2:9-10).**

If you are reading this, you are hungry for the deep things of
God. The Scripture says, **"Deep calls unto deep" (see Psalm
42:7).** This means the depth of your spiritual capacity responds
to the deeper things of God. You are not content with status
quo, mediocre Christianity. Deep does not call to shallowness
or mediocrity; it calls to deep. So, what we learn by the Spirit,
God has prepared and revealed to us. These are the spiritual
treasures for which Christ paid. Spiritual, heavenly realities

and the fullness of the Spirit is our spiritual inheritance as sons and daughters who have access to Christ. The firstborn blessing, which is so important in Hebrew patriarchal culture, contains the authority of God's entire family.

As **"heirs of God and joint heirs with Christ" (see Romans 8:17)**, everything Christ walked in is available to us. Not that we can literally become God, but everything He had as a man—everything we see Jesus do in the Gospels—is made available to us. Spiritual growth brings us to those places in Christ. Being seated with Christ in heavenly places means we do not look at life within the context of this world or from our earthly position, but from our spiritual position in heavenly places in Christ (see Ephesians 1:20). When we pray from our heavenly places, we prophesy from our heavenly places. When we live from that place in the Spirit, we live in an entirely different dimension than those who are not of faith, or who simply operate from their natural, carnal, earthly perspective. "Seated with Christ" also means we are in a posture of rest. We are not striving. Our spiritual treasures and inheritance are revealed to us through His Spirit, which is the sevenfold Spirit of God.

So, we have great capacity for God to reveal things to us. We have great spiritual treasures and a great spiritual inheritance which can only be revealed to us by the sevenfold Holy Spirit. The things the Spirit reveals to us eye cannot see, ear cannot hear, and the natural human heart cannot discern. They are not soulful in nature, but spiritual treasures. Students and friends, please ask God to help you receive what I am sharing with you by faith, so you will know these heavenly realities are available to you by the sevenfold Holy Spirit of God.

The gifts of the Spirit are wonderful. We are not minimizing them, but abiding in His presence with the sevenfold Holy Spirit continually resting on us is far better. Now, what does the activity of the sevenfold Holy Spirit look like in the I Corinthians 2 model where it says, "eye cannot see, nor ear hear, nor can the heart feel?" It doesn't mean we cannot see, hear, or feel some things, or the fruit of these things. In fact, what the sevenfold Holy Spirit *can* reveal to us when we partner with, mature, and grow in Him is profound.

I once had a great encounter with the Lord in which He said, "We are in the time of the Luke 4:18 anointing," which, by the way, has always been available. However, we are now in a season of accelerating this anointing because it's not just a prophetic, healing, or deliverance anointing, but all the above. The Luke 4:18 anointing is the ministry of the Lord Jesus Christ Himself. I want more than just deliverance ministry, evangelistic ministry, or prophetic ministry; I want the ministry of Jesus Christ as found in Luke 4:18.

In 2018, I was given a riddle by the Holy Spirit. When it was given to me, I wrote it down as a note in my iPhone and shared it with many people. The riddle was this: "When the prince shall pass, it will be 4:18 at last." I did not understand what that meant at the time—until it happened. It happened when I was at Mike Bickle's ministry at IHOP in Kansas City in 2021. On April 9, I was on my way to my first session of ministry there when someone told me Prince Philip, Queen Elizabeth's husband, had passed away. It struck me because I remembered the riddle. I shared it that morning and probably gave fifty other prophetic words to people whom I had never met. That was my first time speaking there, and I have been back several times since.

The timeline for Prince Philip's death also became a time marker for the body of Christ and for the greater release of the ministry of Jesus Christ. Prince Philip died on April 9 but was buried on April 18 (4/18). This became a real word from God for that time which spread throughout the body of Christ. Since then, several other connections were made to April 18. For example, Paul Revere's famous ride to warn the Colonial militias of approaching British forces that led to the American Revolutionary War, Martin Luther's trial, and the Doolittle Raid which turned the tide of World War II in the Pacific have all been connected to that date.

Of course, the foundation for Luke 4:18 is Isaiah 61 in the Old Testament. Since this is a prophecy about both the Messiah's first and second coming, the fullness of the Luke 4:18 anointing and the fullness of the ministry of Jesus Christ will not be fully experienced until Christ's second coming or just before. Isaiah 61:1-3: **"The Spirit of the Lord God is upon Me, because the Lord has anointed Me to preach good tidings to the poor; He has sent Me to heal the brokenhearted, to proclaim liberty to the captives, and the opening of the prison to those who are bound; to proclaim the acceptable year of the Lord, and the day of vengeance of our God; to comfort all who mourn, to console those who mourn in Zion, to give them beauty for ashes, the oil of joy for mourning, the garment of praise for the spirit of heaviness; that they may be called the trees of righteousness, the planting of the Lord, that He may be glorified."**

Then in Luke 4:18, Jesus emerged as the Messiah and quoted from Isaiah 61. Now let's compare Isaiah 61:1-2 with Luke 4:18: **"The Spirit of the Lord is upon Me, because He has anointed Me to preach the gospel to the poor, He has**

sent Me to heal the brokenhearted, to proclaim liberty to the captives, and recovery of sight to the blind, to set at liberty those who are oppressed." Notice each of the seven Spirits of God or sevenfold Holy Spirit are involved in the Luke 4:18 anointing and mandate.

Also, notice when Jesus quoted Isaiah 61 in Luke 4:18, He said, **"The Spirit of the Lord is *upon* Me,"** not *in* Me. The Spirit of God was in Him from birth, just as the Spirit of God is in you if you are born again. But there is a clear distinction here between the Spirit of the Lord *in* us versus the Spirit of the Lord *upon* us. The Spirit of the Lord resting on us is what happened to Jesus at His baptism when the Spirit of God descended on Him as a dove and rested or lighted upon Him. This distinction between the Spirit in us and upon us is the difference between where the body of Christ is now. Much of the church has the Spirit in them but not yet upon them as Jesus did from the time of His baptism to His greater ministry of signs, wonders, healings, miracles, prophecy, and deliverance. Though He was born of the Spirit His first thirty years, we did not see any miracles. However, when the Spirit came upon Him, we see this mixture of supernatural ministry, and the same will be true for us. We are desperately in need of a baptism of fire for the Spirit to come upon us. We *must* be filled with the Spirit. The Spirit must come upon us for empowerment, purpose, and for the greater works.

Again, Luke 4:18: **"The Spirit of the Lord is upon Me, because He has anointed Me to preach the gospel to the poor, He has sent Me to heal the brokenhearted, to proclaim liberty to the captives, and recovery of sight to the blind, to set at liberty those who are oppressed."** Many people *want* the anointing but are not fully surrendered or yielded to Jesus to *do* His ministry. Their will is not surrendered to the Father as Jesus' was when He said, **"Not My will, but Yours, be done" (see Luke 22:42)**. Many people want the anointing, but their motives must also be right. If you don't understand the purpose of the anointing, you will forever struggle to get it or try to force it. However, when you align your will with the purposes of God and get the "because" right, the Spirit of the Lord will come upon you and anoint you for specific purposes.

We must have a desire to preach the gospel to the poor, to break the spirit of poverty with all its effects. We must have a desire to heal the brokenhearted, to heal those whose life experiences have left them with a broken heart. We must have a desire to proclaim liberty to the captives, to truly help those who are in bondage. This anointing is in the realm of the Spirit to affect lifestyles and behaviors, to set people free, and to open spiritual eyes. **"Recovery of sight to the blind"** means both spiritual and physical healing. **"To set at liberty those who are oppressed"** is to break the spirit of oppression that binds people. The Luke 4:18 anointing, or sevenfold Holy Spirit of God, is the greatest expression of the ministry of Jesus Christ, and we will soon see this anointing on earth again, and we will be a part of this.

You can respond to this call now to grow into this. The anointing comes when the Spirit rests on us to undo the effects of sin. That is why there are various points of this Luke 4:18 anointing. Sin impoverishes, so we preach the gospel to the poor. Sin breaks people's hearts, so we heal the brokenhearted. Sin makes people captive to many things, so we proclaim liberty to the captives. Sin blinds people, and spiritual blindness is like a veil over people's souls that can include physical blindness, so we proclaim recovery of sight to the blind. Sin oppresses people, so we set at liberty those who are oppressed.

Jesus said, **"Today this Scripture is fulfilled in your hearing" (see Luke 4:21).** He fulfilled it. Then He told us we could do the works that He did, and the works that He did were a result of this Luke 4:18 anointing. The ministry of Jesus Christ is when we mature beyond the nine gifts of the Spirit to the sevenfold Spirit of God. Understand this is a new level of ministry directly connected to the ministry of the Lord Jesus Christ called the Luke 4:18 anointing, the sevenfold Holy Spirit of God, or the nine gifts of the Spirit in full maturity.

Truly, if we are not breaking poverty over people through the power and anointing of the abiding Holy Spirit, if we are not breaking poverty spirits, mindsets, and generational poverty, if we are not healing the brokenhearted, setting the captives free, restoring spiritual and physical blindness, and setting at liberty those who are oppressed, our ministries are probably off course. If our focus is on other things, then our focus is not right. **"The Spirit of the Lord is upon Me *because* He has anointed Me to…."** Many people want more anointing, but we must get the "because" right. The sevenfold Holy Spirit will produce the ministry of Jesus Christ in the earth in a greater measure when we get our "because" right.

Though Jesus quoted Isaiah 61 in Luke 4:18, He intentionally left something out in Luke 4:19. He said, **"To proclaim the acceptable year of the Lord,"** but then left out, **"and the day of vengeance of our God."** I believe He left that out because **"the day of vengeance of our God"** is reserved for His second coming. It's still a part of the Isaiah 61/Luke 4:18 dynamic, but Luke 4:18 is the first coming of Christ, while the fullness of Isaiah 61 won't be experienced until the second coming of Christ and the events leading up to it, which I believe we are approaching. We are certainly closer now than we were last year. So, if a part of Isaiah 61:1-3 is not listed in Luke 4:18-19 associated with His first coming, it must mean this anointing will reemerge in a highlighted way or larger scale leading up to or associated with His second coming.

Now you can understand how this message of the seven Spirits of God is intricately tied to Isaiah 61 and Luke 4:18. As we near the second coming of Christ, we will see another fulfillment of Isaiah 61/Luke 4:18 to complete it. This is the company of overcomers who will do the greater works and demonstrate the powers of the age to come just before the second coming in fulfillment of Scripture. No longer will we operate in the down payment or earnest of our inheritance of which Paul spoke, which happened at Pentecost, and which we still walk in now. Instead, we will operate in the fullness of the sevenfold Spirit of God in fulfillment of the Isaiah 61/ Luke 4:18 mandate. Another layer and greater fulfillment of this mandate has been reserved for this hour, and you are called to be part of it. If you did not feel called, you would not be reading this.

We find each of the seven Spirits of God in the Isaiah 61/ Luke 4:18 mandate. The fullness of the Holy Spirit and the sevenfold Spirit are needed to accomplish the "becauses" of Luke 4:18 to break the spirit of poverty, heal the broken-hearted, set at liberty those who are bound by drugs and addictions, recover spiritual and physical sight through divine healing, set at liberty those who are oppressed, and proclaim the acceptable year of the Lord. The time is now. Not next year or the year after, this year. This is our year to rise to our full inheritance—not just having the Spirit fill us but having the abiding Holy Spirit rest on us as He did at Christ's baptism, inaugurating His supernatural ministry, which He prophesied we would also do—the greater works. The powers of the age to come happening in this age will be the nine gifts of the Spirit in full maturity or the sevenfold Holy Spirit of God.

If something is leaping or resonating in your spirit right now, it is because this is the mandate and commission the Lord has placed on me: to lead an end-time company of people into the Isaiah 61/Luke 4:18 greater works. Incidentally, that prophecy about Prince Philip dying was not only a time marker to tell the body of Christ Luke 4:18 was about to increase in the earth, but it was also when my ministry began to accelerate. This is the mandate and purpose for my life and ministry: to help lead this company of people who feel called to step out of mediocre Christianity and step into the fullness of the sevenfold Holy Spirit, to demonstrate the Isaiah 61/Luke 4:18 greater works and powers of the age to come, to train and equip a company of people who will learn how to walk in this, and to go from being filled with the Spirit to having the Spirit rest on us, just like at Christ's baptism.

The seven Spirits are necessary for the fulfillment of Luke 4:18. Notice in Isaiah 11:2, which names the seven Spirits, as well as on the menorah, there are three couplings. The Spirit of the Lord is like the middle pillar of the menorah, then there are three branches which represent the Tree of Life having branches and anointing oil that flow through the branches to produce flames of fire. Those three couplings are the Spirit of wisdom and understanding, the Spirit of counsel and might, and the Spirit of knowledge and the fear of the Lord. Each has two candlesticks connected by the same oil that produces the flames. The same oil that produces the flame of the Spirit of wisdom produces the flame of the Spirit of understanding. The same oil that fuels the flame of the Spirit of counsel fuels the flame of the Spirit of might. The same anointing oil that flows into the Spirit of knowledge also flows into the Spirit of the fear of the Lord. These three couplings, or six Spirits, work in direct partnership with one another to accomplish specific purposes.

Now, since the Spirit of wisdom is found throughout Scripture going back to creation, there is much to learn. The Spirit of wisdom comes after the Spirit of the Lord. The Spirit of the Lord speaks generally of the Lord's presence or atmosphere. The other six that follow the Spirit of the Lord complete the Spirit of God, including His actions and activities. When the Spirit of wisdom rests upon you, it flows like a river, showing you what to do in every situation—what to say, what not to say, what to do, and what not to do. Wisdom teaches us how to correctly apply the revelation we receive, which is the Spirit of revelation or understanding. Revelation and understanding partners with and is coupled to wisdom. Without revelation, it is just wisdom. The Spirit of wisdom gives us a discerning heart to know what, when, and how to do things. The Spirit of wisdom is the Spirit of the Lord giving us the know-how and the right words to properly communicate the revelation we receive.

The Scripture says, Jesus **"grew in spirit, filled with wisdom" (see Luke 2:40)**. This may mean natural wisdom, but we know He eventually had the abiding Spirit of wisdom as well. There is also a difference between the gift of a word of wisdom and the Spirit of wisdom. The Spirit of wisdom is an abiding, continual anointing, not a come-and-go gift.

Deuteronomy 34:9 says, **"Now Joshua the son of Nun was full of the spirit of wisdom, for Moses had laid his hands on him; so the children of Israel heeded him, and did as the Lord had commanded Moses."** When you have that Spirit of wisdom, people will look to you. There will be a real trust in your ability to discern circumstances, to make right decisions, and to choose correct responses. In this Old Testament example, the Spirit of wisdom was imparted. Joshua received the Spirit of wisdom by impartation when Moses laid hands on him.

The benefits of wisdom are incredible, especially when they come from the Spirit. In II Chronicles 1:7-12, the Lord appeared to Solomon and said, **"Ask! What shall I give you?"** Now I cannot imagine a better position to be in than for God to say, "Ask what you will, and I will give it to you." Solomon could have asked for and received many things, but he had asked for wisdom, realizing that wisdom could bring many other things, like riches and authority. Solomon said, **"'Now give me wisdom and knowledge, that I may go out and come in before this people; for who can judge this great people of Yours?' Then God said to Solomon: 'Because this was in your heart, and you have not asked riches or wealth or honor or the life of your enemies, nor have you asked long life—but have asked wisdom and knowledge for yourself, that you may judge My people over whom I have made you king—wisdom and knowledge are granted to you; and I will give you riches and wealth and honor, such as none of the kings had who were before you, nor shall any after you have the like.'"**

The Luke 4:18 anointing comes because it is in your heart to do something for God. Solomon had a right to the Spirit of wisdom because he wanted to judge God's people. Consequently, the Spirit of wisdom and knowledge were granted to him. The Spirit of wisdom was given to Solomon because it was for the right cause and right motive. This gave him the right to ask for wisdom. Then the Lord told him riches, wealth, and honor would also be given to him because his heart was right, and because he did not ask for them. Thus, to this day, Solomon is considered the wisest man who ever lived.

After the Queen of Sheba came and learned of Solomon's wisdom and riches, **"Then she said to the king: 'It was a true report which I heard in my own land about your words and your wisdom. However I did not believe their words until I came and saw with my own eyes; and indeed the half of the greatness of your wisdom was not told me. You exceed the fame of which I heard'"** (II Chronicles 1:5-6). Solomon desired to rule well and to judge matters fairly and accurately, and God was pleased with his request because it not only benefited him but also served the greater good of the nation. Consequently, God could also trust him with riches, honor, prestige, and recognition. Wisdom brings wealth, honor, and instruction.

Proverbs 1:2-3 says, **"To know wisdom and instruction, to perceive the words of understanding, to receive the instruction of wisdom."** What does it look like to **"receive the instruction of wisdom"**? Wisdom teaches us through life's everyday moments; not only in crises, but also in everything we do. Wisdom teaches us how to apply knowledge and revelation from the Bible to every situation. We know the Bible instructs and is full of wisdom and knowledge, yet many people never extrapolate its truths or apply them to their lives. Perhaps they are missing the Spirit of wisdom. The Spirit of wisdom allows you to extract the gold. Through the Spirit of wisdom, we know the Bible was not only written to us but also for us, so we can obtain wisdom from the Scriptures, parables, and stories, and apply them to our present-day lives and circumstances. The Spirit of wisdom enables us to extract hidden wisdom, knowledge, revelation, and truth, which most people miss by surface reading, and apply it to our lives.

Wisdom is a Spirit. It is the Spirit of the Lord, but it is only one part of the Spirit of the Lord. Proverbs 1:20-23 says, **"Wisdom calls aloud outside; she raises her voice in the open squares. She cries out in the chief concourses, at the openings of the gates in the city, she speaks her words: 'How long, you simple ones, will you love simplicity? For scorners delight in their scorning, and fools hate knowledge. Turn at my rebuke; surely I will pour out my Spirit on you; I will make my words known to you."** Notice wisdom can pour out of her Spirit. This is a remarkable invitation. Can you hear the cry? Can you discern it? Can you hear the still, small voice of the Holy Spirit, the Spirit of wisdom? This cry and invitation have now been extended to us.

Notice the Spirit of wisdom is personified here as a female messenger. Not to imply that the Spirit of God is female, but many times the Scriptures speak of how God created man before the woman, and that the woman was in the man and was taken out of the man. So, when God created man in His image, the woman was in the man, then created from his rib. Thus, the image of God is the fullness of male and female, the lion and the lamb, the Father and the Son. In other words, in the fullness of God we see both authority and submission.

Notice the Spirit of wisdom is trying to get the attention of the simple ones, who relish in their simplicity but never grow, mature, or advance in life. They are content with their simplicity. Of course, we don't want to overcomplicate things unnecessarily. But in this case, wisdom says, you need more wisdom than what you have. Don't be content with simplicity. You need the Spirit of the Lord and the wisdom of the Lord. Wisdom brings long life. Proverbs 4:5 says, **"Get wisdom! Get understanding! Do not forget, nor turn away from the words of my mouth."**

Then in the New Testament, we also see these two, the spirit of wisdom and understanding or revelation, coupled together. Ephesians 1:17, **"That the God of our Lord Jesus Christ, the Father of glory, may give to you the spirit of wisdom and revelation in the knowledge of Him."** All seven Spirits of God are mentioned here in Ephesians 1, as Paul prayed that God would give the ones to whom he was writing the Spirit of wisdom and revelation. Paul essentially prayed that the church would experience the seven Spirits of God, the Spirit of wisdom and revelation, by knowing Christ deeply and intimately.

Now Proverbs 3:13-18, **"Happy is the man who finds wisdom, and the man who gains understanding; for her proceeds are better than the profits of silver, and her gain than fine gold. She is more precious than rubies, and all the things you may desire cannot compare with her. Length of days is in her right hand, in her left hand riches and honor. Her ways are ways of pleasantness, and all her paths are peace. She is a tree of life to those who take hold of her, and happy are all who retain her."**

To find something, you must first look for it. If you want to experience true happiness, find wisdom. If you find the Spirit of wisdom, you will experience not only riches and honor but also longer life. If you want more peace in your life, find wisdom. Most anxieties people deal with happen because the path they are walking is not in the Spirit of wisdom. I realize this is a blanket statement, but most of the fears, anxieties, and uncertainties we walk in are the result of being unsure what wisdom would have us do.

Remember, the menorah, which is in the Holy Place, is a picture of the Tree of Life. From the beginning, God desired man not to live from the knowledge of good and evil but from the Tree of Life. He wanted us to live by the Spirit, teach by the Spirit, learn by the Spirit, and do everything by the Spirit. The menorah even looks like a tree with branches. **"Her ways are ways of pleasantness, and all her paths are peace. She is a tree of life to those who take hold of her and happy are all who retain her."** Don't just find wisdom. Don't just have a dating relationship with wisdom. Marry her, stay with her, and retain her.

The Spirit of wisdom is also different from ordinary wisdom because it comes from the realm of the Spirit. It is inspiration that comes from the Spirit. When you are inspired by the Spirit of wisdom to know what to do or say, there is an endless source and flow of inspiration. The Spirit brings wisdom. This is not intellectual knowledge or wisdom that comes from reading books. That is a form of wisdom, but you can also gain wisdom from the Spirit, which you cannot gain from learning or reading.

The Bible prophesies of a time, which we are soon approaching, when the people of God will know more by the Spirit than they will know by reading, education, or intellect. Many things we are currently doing through education and learning we will learn through the fullness of the sevenfold Spirit. No more will a man teach his neighbor or brother saying, "Know the Lord," but all shall know Him, from the least to the greatest (see Hebrews 8:11). People will learn more by the Spirit than they will by teaching. Not that we will no longer need teaching, but wouldn't it be great if we taught and learned everything by the Spirit? Everything we have now we learn by reading, hearing, and teaching. What if we had a source like a river in which everything came to us by the Spirit of wisdom? She is a tree of life to those who take hold of her. That means we can eat from and be sustained by this tree.

Proverbs 3:19 says, **"The Lord by wisdom founded the earth; by understanding He established the heavens."** Here we again see wisdom and understanding coupled together. In fact, in Proverbs 8, we can see all seven Spirits of God listed together, even at creation, just as in Isaiah 11:2. Of course, the sevenfold Holy Spirit was there at creation. God is a Spirit. When God said in Genesis 1:26, **"Let Us make man in Our image, according to Our likeness,"** I believe He was speaking to the seven Spirits of God. When God created man a spiritual being with a spirit, soul, and body, He distinguished him from the plant and animal kingdoms. By making mankind in His image and likeness, He made us spiritual beings. God is also a Spirit. Our human spirit comes from Him. But when God said, **"Let Us make man in Our image,"** He was also consulting with the seven Spirits of God. We know this because Ephesians 1:11 tells us the Lord **"works all things according to the counsel of His will."**

Proverbs 8 proves beyond a shadow of doubt that God spoke to the seven Spirits of God at creation:

"Does not wisdom cry out, and understanding lift up her voice?

She takes her stand on the top of the high hill, beside the way, where the paths meet.

She cries out by the gates, at the entry of the city. At the entrance of the doors:

'To you, O men, I call, and my voice is to the sons of men.

O you simple ones, understand prudence, and you fools, be of an understanding heart.

Listen, for I will speak of excellent things, and from the opening of my lips will come right things;

for my mouth will speak truth; wickedness is an abomination to my lips.

All the words in my mouth are with righteousness; nothing crooked or perverse is in them. They are all plain to him who understands, and right to those who find knowledge.

Receive my instruction and not silver, and knowledge rather than choice gold;

for wisdom is better than rubies, and all the things one may desire cannot be compared with her.

I, wisdom, dwell with prudence, and find out knowledge and discretion.

The fear of the Lord is to hate evil. Pride and arrogance and the evil way and the perverse mouth I hate.

Counsel is mine, and sound wisdom; I am understanding, I have strength [might].

By me kings reign, and rulers decree justice.

By me princes rule, and nobles, all the judges of the earth.

I love those who love me, and those who seek me diligently will find me.

Riches and honor are with me, enduring riches and righteousness.

My fruit is better than gold, yes, than fine gold, and my revenue than choice silver.

I traverse the way of righteousness in the midst of the paths of justice,

that I may cause those who love me to inherit wealth, that I may fill their treasuries.

The Lord possessed me at the beginning of His way, before His works of old.

I have been established from everlasting, from the beginning, before there was ever an earth.

When there were no depths I was brought forth, when there were no fountains abounding with water.

Before the mountains were settled, before the hills, I was brought forth;

while as yet He had not made the earth or the fields, or the primal dust of the world.

When He prepared the heavens, I was there, when He drew a circle on the face of the deep,

when He established the clouds above, when he strengthened the fountains of the deep,

when He assigned to the sea its limit, so that the waters would not transgress His command, when He marked out the foundations of the earth,

then I was beside Him as a master craftsman; and I was daily His delight, rejoicing always before Him,

rejoicing in His inhabited world, and my delight was with the sons of men.

Now therefore, listen to me, my children, for blessed are those who keep my ways.

Hear instruction and be wise, and do not disdain it.

Blessed is the man who listens to me, watching daily at my gates, waiting at the post of my doors.

For whoever find me finds life, and obtains favor from the Lord;

but he who sins against me wrongs his own soul; all those who hate me love death.'"

Proverbs 8 lists all seven Spirits of God by name, and they all go back with the Lord at creation. So, when the Lord said, **"Let Us make man in Our image,"** He was speaking to those other six Spirits. Wisdom said, "I was with the Lord at the beginning." That's the seventh Spirit, the Spirit of wisdom, referring to the Lord Himself. All seven Spirits are mentioned, just as in Isaiah 11:2.

So now we understand Genesis 1:1-3: **"In the beginning God created the heavens and the earth. The earth was without form, and void; and darkness was on the face of the deep. And the Spirit of God was hovering over the face of the waters. Then God said, 'Let there be light…'"** The very first time the Spirit of God is mentioned in Genesis with the voice of God at creation, the seven Spirits of God were there, because the Spirit of God *is* the seven Spirits, and *seven* means "complete." The Spirit of God was hovering there over the waters because the Lord "was working all things according to the counsel of His own will." He looked within Himself, like the kings of the Old Testament who would look themselves in the mirror and decree, "Let us do this." The seven Spirits were His royal decree. Don't you do that yourself? Don't you look in the mirror and say, "Let's see, what are we going to do today?" You're consulting with your own wisdom, counsel, and knowledge to decide what you will do that day.

So, raise your level of desire for the Spirit of wisdom, and raise your spirit of expectation for the Spirit of wisdom. To activate the Spirit of wisdom in your life, pray this prayer out loud: *"Father God, in the name of our Lord Jesus Christ, I ask as Solomon of old asked, please grant me the wisdom and knowledge needed, and particularly the Spirit of wisdom. Let it become a tree of life to me, to feed and sustain my life. Lord, I ask for a supernatural impartation of the Spirit of wisdom, the same Spirit of wisdom that guided You in the creation of the world. Let it also guide me and take me to new levels of authority, accomplishment, and purpose on the earth. In the name of Jesus Christ, amen."*

CHAPTER 4

The Spirit of Understanding (Revelation)

Those who are prophetic will especially appreciate the Spirit of revelation, or understanding, among the seven Spirits. Revelation, or understanding, means to bring light to hidden things. If you were to walk in a dark room where there are no lights, stub your toe on the couch, and run into the table, you might wonder what the point is of wandering in the dark. Then, you would go back and flip on the light switch. Everything in the room, including the couch and table, would not just suddenly appear. Instead, the light would only reveal what was there all along. You just couldn't see them until the light was turned on.

The same is true regarding the Spirit of understanding, or the Spirit of revelation. There are hidden treasures the Lord loves to reveal to us, so we can understand His ways. Identifying these are very important. The Spirit of revelation can literally remove a veil from our eyes when we read the Bible. You may have read the same chapter several, or even a hundred times, and not understood it, yet when the Spirit of revelation turns on, suddenly you understand everything you previously did not understand. The Holy Spirit brings revelation and illumination.

There are two types of revelation in Scripture worth distinguishing. When the Bible speaks of the Spirit of revelation or understanding, many people think that means understanding the Bible. That is a type of revelation, but another type of revelation comes through prophetic experiences such as dreams, trances, or supernatural encounters. These are also very real and precious experiences.

The first type of revelation mentioned in Scripture is in Job 33:14-16: **"For God may speak in one way, or in another, yet man does not perceive it. In a dream, in a vision of the night, when deep sleep falls upon men, while slumbering on their beds, then He opens the ears of men, and seals their instruction."** God speaks to us in many ways, yet many do not perceive it. I spend much of my time in ministry teaching people how to identify the voice of God or how to identify their prophetic filter. God will use our knowledge, experiences, and basically anything He can to relate and speak to us. We see this throughout Scripture where God understood and used unique, parabolic languages to speak to specific persons or groups.

For instance, when He would speak to a baker in the Bible through a dream or a prophetic message, He would speak in terms of bread or baskets of bread because that was something they could relate to and understand. When He would speak to farmers, He would speak in agrarian terms, like ears of corn, seed, or soil. God often uses unique terms and languages to speak to His people.

When Job said, **"God may speak in one way, or another, yet man does not perceive,"** have you ever wondered how many times God spoke to you, yet you did not realize it? Perhaps you thought that was just your own mind speaking, a pizza dream, or an ordinary experience. No, that was God speaking to you! God communicates to us through His still, small voice—through promptings, nudges, and any other way He can—yet we often don't perceive it. We need to learn to recognize the many ways God speaks to us. We may not always perceive them, but in a dream, or in a vision of the night, when deep sleep falls on us, He opens our ears and seals our instruction.

Why does God speak to us through dreams? Because when we sleep, our conscious minds shut down, so God doesn't have to filter through all that brain chatter as He does when we're awake. He can bypass our conscious minds and go straight to our subconscious minds through dreams, parables, and stories. He will even use a message with symbols to which we can relate. God can speak to us in many ways through dreams.

I have had dreams in which the Spirit of revelation spoke to me, and I would know the night before about someone I would see the next day. I knew what they were going to say, what they needed to know, or what was happening in their lives. Even if I was planning to meet them, the Spirit of revelation would come in my sleep and show me something beforehand. I would tell them a day or two or a week later when I saw them, and they would be blown away. "How did you know that?" "How did you know I was going through that?" "How did you know that was a need in my life?" God seals our instruction.

So, dreams and visions are one way God speaks. In Acts, Simon Peter fell into a trance on a rooftop. He saw in the trance a vision of a sheet coming down from heaven with all kinds of creatures on it. When you read it, you think, what a bizarre way to communicate. He sees all these creatures coming down on a sheet, and the takeaway is that the gospel can now be preached to the Gentiles. How did he get that out of that? To understand, we would need to know the symbolic and parabolic languages in which God speaks.

Rarely does the Spirit of God speak audibly. He does, but not frequently, because a spirit does not have flesh and bones. Jesus said, **"That which is born of the flesh is flesh, and that which is born of the Spirit is spirit" (see John 3:6).** A spirit also does not have vocal cords. The Holy Spirit can speak, but He is not likely to speak audibly. So, we learn to hear the voice of God through dreams, trances, strong impressions, feelings, etc.

God can even communicate revelation to us through our senses. **"Oh, taste and see that the Lord is good" (see Psalm 34:8).** We can taste His goodness as well as see His goodness. We can even smell His goodness. Proverbs and the Song of Songs speak much of fragrances and smells that can communicate revelation truth by the Spirit of God to our senses and can be used to communicate God's will to us.

Others have been caught up in heavenly experiences. The Bible is full of godly encounters that changed the courses and trajectories of peoples' lives. Those who teach that we do not need the prophetic, or that it was reserved only for the first century, must remove most of the Bible to remove all the Holy Spirit's gifts and workings. Few, if any, pages would remain. It's so sad to see the Christianity that most people are experiencing. They think they can know the Lord intimately simply by reading about Him, but they cannot (see John 5:39).

The Spirit of revelation can communicate to us through visions, dreams, and imagery to convey messages. Each person must learn to develop their own unique prophetic filter and way in which God relates to them based on their own personality and experiences. The more you learn to identify His voice, the more you will learn to hear His voice.

The second type of revelation in Scripture, after prophetic revelation, is divine revelation. How can we know the difference? Have you ever just known something, but no one told you about it, and you never saw or heard of it, you just knew it? First, that is *not* the gift of discernment or suspicion. Some people think they know many things that may or may not be true. Their conspiracy mindedness convinces them it is true, whether it's true or not. Now if your conspiracy mindedness or suspicion level is true, then yes, God is speaking to you, and you can know whether something is true.

When I first started ministering prophetically, I knew this had to have been something with which I was born. Like Jeremiah, **"Before I formed you in the womb I knew you; before you were born I sanctified you; I ordained you a prophet to the nations" (Jeremiah 1:5)**. As I look back over my life as a young man, I realize I had many encounters with the Lord for which I did not even have a grid.

I now know these were prophetic experiences, but many times before I started seeing visions, I was consistently praying and being shown when someone had cancer, or I would see people at their doctor's appointments and hear what the doctor had told them. So, I knew how to pray for people, or give them a word of knowledge, or a prophetic word. But before all that developed, I just knew things. I knew when someone had a heart condition. Then I started testing, verifying, trusting, and acting on what I knew, and God started trusting me with more extensive revelation.

So, it's important to understand the difference between prophetic and divine revelation. Divine revelation is when you suddenly realize something that can be confirmed by Scripture. It might be a "déjà vu" experience where you suddenly remembered you had a previous or similar experience and somehow instinctively knew what to do. Often certain feelings are associated with those experiences.

The apostle Paul wrote much about the Spirit of wisdom and revelation, but he also wrote about a continuing revelation, which is how he wrote more than half of the New Testament. Though he was not taught by Jesus nor part of Jesus' earthly ministry, or even taught by Peter or one of the apostles, he later met and spoke with the apostles and confirmed that what God had taught him by revelation was indeed correct.

Galatians 1:11-12: **"But I make known to you, brethren, that the gospel which was preached by me is not according to man. For I neither received it from man, nor was I taught it, but it came through the revelation of Jesus Christ."** This is a perfect example of learning by revelation, from the Tree of Life instead of the Tree of the Knowledge of Good and Evil.

This dynamic was presented to man in the beginning, but we chose to learn knowledge, wisdom, and instruction from the Tree of the Knowledge of Good and Evil instead. The serpent said to the woman, **"For God knows that in the day you eat of it, your eyes will be open, and you will be like God, knowing good and evil" (Genesis 3:5).** This immediately made her feel deprived if she did not partake of the Tree of the Knowledge of Good and Evil.

This is also a prophetic picture of the two covenants. The Tree of the Knowledge of Good and Evil is a picture of the old covenant. In the law, we were told what was good and evil, but it did not produce life or power in us. It only revealed sin and what was right and wrong. Man could not live up to the law because he was trying to do good and trying not to do evil based on knowledge instead of by the power of the Holy Spirit. The Tree of Life is a picture of the new covenant, in which we walk in revelation and understanding of things we did not learn from others or by reading.

The Spirit of revelation will never disagree with God's written Word but will always confirm the written Word. Still, there are many things God wants to teach us by knowing and understanding by the Spirit. Not by reading or by someone telling us, but instead, like Paul, "we received it not from man, nor were we taught it, but it came through the revelation of Jesus Christ." It came by the Tree of Life, not by the Tree of the Knowledge of Good and Evil.

Again, Paul said in Ephesians 3:3-4, **"How that by revelation He made known to me the mystery (as I have briefly written already, by which, when you read, you may understand my knowledge in the mystery of Christ)."** Paul's knowledge came by revelation, not from books, schooling, or education. That is why Paul's ministry was so consequential and why he wrote more than half the New Testament. The Spirit of revelation wants to teach us the hidden mysteries of God and His Word, not through man's knowledge or through written texts.

Paul continues in Ephesians 3:5, **"Which in other ages was not made known to the sons of men, as it has been now revealed by the Spirit to His holy apostles and prophets."** You can receive knowledge by revelation. You can receive things by revelation you did not understand before, even things you could not fully grasp by reading or watching a program. When you receive it by revelation, it is impartation.

Paul also wrote in Ephesians 1:17, **"That the God of our Lord Jesus Christ, the Father of glory, may give to you the spirit of wisdom, and revelation in the knowledge of Him."** Remember, the Spirit of wisdom and revelation are coupled and work in tandem together. Revelation comes by the Spirit, then the Spirit of wisdom helps you appropriate and apply the revelation you received. This puts you on the cutting edge and allows you to be one step ahead of those who do not walk in the power of the Holy Spirit.

Paul continues in Ephesians 1:18-19, **"The eyes of your understanding being enlightened; that you may know what is the hope of His calling, what are the riches of the glory of His inheritance in the saints, and what is the exceeding greatness of His power toward us who believe, according to the working of His mighty power."** We desperately need the Spirit of revelation, and what revelation shows you, the Spirit of wisdom helps you apply. Without the Spirit of wisdom, you won't know what to do with divine revelation.

This happened throughout history: men and women of God received real revelation from God, but they did not have the wisdom to know how to apply or share it. So, it ended up in the wrong hands, and many dangerous cults and groups emerged. So, they began right by identifying the revelation from God, but then took it beyond its boundaries by not properly interpreting and applying it. Delivery, timing, and application of revelation are so vitally important. That's what the Spirit of wisdom does for the Spirit of revelation. It helps us with understanding, interpretation, delivery, timing, and application of that revelation. Wisdom knows how to appropriate it.

The provisions God brings through the Spirits of wisdom and revelation, according to Ephesians 1:17, come through the riches of His glory. Wisdom and revelation teach us how to receive supernatural provisions and how to take full advantage of our inheritance through Christ's work on the cross. We cannot fully know our inheritance nor what is available to us without the Spirit of wisdom and revelation. Without wisdom and revelation, we cannot even understand who we are or our glorious inheritance in Christ. Consequently, many Christians do not know who they are and what they have and, sadly, live far below their privilege.

Revelation must be tempered. Without proper balance, an abundance of revelations can lead to pride. Paul understood this and knew how to partner with the Spirit of wisdom and revelation. Revelation must also be held in check by the motives of our hearts and by how we receive and process things by the Spirit of revelation. **"And lest I should be exalted above**

measure, by the abundance of the revelations, a thorn in the flesh was given to me, a messenger of Satan to buffet me, lest I be exalted above measure" (II Corinthians 12:7). The key phrase here is "above measure."

When we become so highly exalted that we think we are above the actual revelation, we are operating in presumption. The revelation is ground zero. When we get so excited about it that we rise above this level, we become exalted above measure or above the revelation we were given. It's one thing to acknowledge that God has given us revelation, process it, and even share it, but when we let ourselves become exalted above that revelation, we open ourselves to spiritual attacks. For this reason, in services where the Spirit of revelation comes on me, I may give two, three, or four prophetic words but rarely go beyond that.

When we start giving specific, detailed words to someone about a dream they had, or what it meant, or bring the word of the Lord to them and they confirm it, they know we could not have known that by natural means. This may be a prophetic dream from the Lord about a sibling, a disease, or a secret of their heart, but when people start admiring us in unhealthy ways because of our revelation, we can become exalted within ourselves, or they can exalt us above the measure of that revelation. That's when things can get out of hand.

That is also when we get out from under God's covering and protection. When the measure of exaltation we receive from ourselves and others exceeds the level of revelation, we will start hearing or receiving backlash or disparaging remarks against us. The distance between those two points can become dangerous. Our level of revelation must be commensurate with our level of exaltation. When these two become widely separated, we become open prey for the enemy, and if you have ever been through that, it's torturous.

Often a "messenger of Satan" can benefit you. I think Paul's "messenger of Satan" was a person, not a sickness or a disease, and I think it was someone who constantly reminded him of his humanity, but because he was so anointed and gifted prophetically, that bothered him. Evidently, there was someone there with Paul who kept him humble and made sure there was not a wide gap between his level of exaltation and level of revelation.

When these two stay commensurate, we are safe. When we only speak what the Lord gives us, we are safe. So long as our hearts do not get puffed up beyond what the Lord said, we are safe. We are covered because we operate in grace. Sometimes, with the abundance of revelation, people will say, "Wow, that was incredible!" However, revelation is not about entertainment but about purpose.

There have been times when I have received prophetic words or foreseen events or predicted something months or years beforehand that came to pass, but I always remained transparent and vulnerable about them. Though the prophetic has been attacked harshly by certain communities, I have never felt the need to step in and become a "bodyguard" for the prophetic by flaunting my prophetic words to try and validate the prophetic community at large. Sometimes the Lord will allow us to experience a humbling through these messengers. Even if our motives are not to exalt ourselves, God does not need us to defend His prophetic gifts. God has a way of working those things out, and one "thorn in the flesh" is plenty. We don't need a company of them.

I have found this to be true time and again: We must make sure our brokenness and humility before the Lord keep our hearts and postures right according to the revelation we receive. Paul experienced many trials and external scenarios which he specifically named: stripes, beatings, stonings, shipwrecks, perils, hardships, and fasts. All these have a way of keeping us tethered to earth and to reality, so we don't think of ourselves more highly than we ought to think (see Romans 12:3). As we grow in revelation, these are all very real things we must manage within ourselves.

Just because we receive a revelation that turns out to be true or comes to pass and people are blessed by it, if not careful, our hearts can be puffed up. When we finally get a sense of appreciation for our ministry gifts, and people start noticing us, we must guard our hearts to remain pure and right before the Lord.

Paul was certainly successful in the prophetic. He talked about the high level of revelation he received in II Corinthians 12:2: **"I know a man in Christ, who fourteen years ago—whether in the body I do not know, or whether out of the body I do not know, God knows—how he was caught up into Paradise and heard inexpressible words, which it is not lawful for a man to utter."** Paul described himself and his experience in the third person. Why? He did not want to unduly draw attention to himself. He did not want his level of exaltation to exceed his level of revelation. The more honorable and humble we are with the revelation God gives us, the more revelation with which he can trust us.

Paul continued: **"Therefore I take pleasure in infirmities, in reproaches, in needs, in persecutions, in distresses,**

for Christ's sake. For when I am weak, then I am strong" **(II Corinthians 12:10).** Do you know anyone who can honestly say, "I take pleasure in weaknesses and reproaches"? Do you know anyone who rejoices when difficult times, persecutions, and needs arise? If you do, that person likely walks on the same level of revelation as the apostle Paul. Paul knew that danger, backlash, and spiritual warfare could result were he to become "highly exalted." That is why he took pleasure in infirmities.

When our health fails, should we take pleasure in that? When reproach comes and people criticize and talk about us, or when needs arise and we can barely pay our bills or make ends meet, when we are distressed and life becomes overwhelming, should we take pleasure in that? How could Paul take pleasure in that? Because he knew that was what kept him grounded and tethered to reality.

Paul did not want to become exalted above measure or discontented with who he was, like Lucifer with all his diamonds, beautiful coverings, and authority. The Scripture says, because of his beauty and position, he exalted himself (see Isaiah 14:12-14). It came to the point where he started to believe all the nice things the angels said about him and thought he could even exalt his throne above God's throne. His ego was way out of control, and because of this, he was cast down from heaven, lost his privileges with God, and led a rebellion of angels who were also cast out.

He was the first whose level of exaltation exceeded his level of spiritual authority. This is one of the most important lessons we can learn in life: When we are out of bounds and our level of exaltation exceeds our level of authority, we not only want God to humble us, but we also want to take pleasure in trials.

When we learn to keep our joy even when being ridiculed, getting rejected, having our health fail, seeing our friends and enemies be against us, struggling financially, feeling under pressure, being stressed, and having life pull us apart—that is when God can give us more revelation. That is because we **"have learned in whatever state we are, to be content" (see Philippians 4:11)**.

The Spirit of revelation and understanding, as one of the seven Spirits of God, is incredible. But more importantly, we must learn to develop our spiritual and emotional maturity to where we can enjoy life, even when everything is upside down. When stress, persecution, and infirmities can cause us to react or become miserable, our hearts are no longer right with the Lord. We lose our joy and victory in the Lord. When changing or negative circumstances can cause our faith in God to become weakened, our love for the Lord is not where it should be. Such circumstances reveal we need more than revelation. We need to learn how to be content and joyful in any state, because one day, we just might end up writing letters under candlelight in a dark dungeon that will be read by Christians for thousands of years.

In the end, this is the most important truth and reality prophetic people must develop. We must never allow our circumstances, distresses, persecutions, infirmities, or lack cause us to explode with spiritual frustration and anger. When we respond to difficult circumstances in this way, it reveals our level of exaltation is above our level of revelation. When we find ourselves going into protection mode saying things like,

"I can't believe this is happening to me," or "I can't let you do this to me," or "I can't believe life is so unfair," we need to guard our hearts (see Proverbs 4:23; Philippians 4:7). Never allow the negative circumstances of the moment supersede the truth of God's Word, who He is, and who we are in Him.

CHAPTER 5

The Spirit of Counsel and Might

The Spirit of counsel and might is the second coupling mentioned in Isaiah 11:2: **"The Spirit of the Lord will rest upon Him** [Jesus]**, the Spirit of wisdom and understanding, the Spirit of counsel and might, the Spirit of knowledge and of the fear of the Lord."** Of all the seven Spirits of God, or sevenfold Holy Spirit, the Spirit of counsel and might is my favorite. Since this is a coupling that is rarely seen in Scripture without the other, we will look at them together. The Spirit of counsel is simply God's advice for a plan of action, but not acting on it until we have waited on the Lord. The Spirit of counsel shows us what to do, so we can do it. Rest assured the Spirit of might will bring it to pass. It's not anything we do; we just show up. **"Not by might nor by power, but by My Spirit, says the Lord of hosts" (see Zechariah 4:6).** In short, the Spirit of counsel is listening for God's plan of action to meet a need or situation.

Joshua 6 is one of the most incredible passages in the Bible and a great example of the Spirit of counsel and might. **"And the Lord said to Joshua: 'See! I have given Jericho into** your hand, its king, and the mighty men of valor. You shall march around the city, all you men of war; you shall go all around the city once. This you shall do six days. And seven priests shall bear seven trumpets of rams' horns before the ark. But the seventh day you shall march around the city seven times, and the priests shall blow the trumpets. It shall come to pass, when they make a long blast with the ram's horn, and when you hear the sound of the trumpet, that all the people shall shout with a great shout; then the wall of the city will fall down flat. And the people shall go up every man straight before him.' Then Joshua the son of Nun called the priests and said to them, 'Take up the ark of the covenant, and let seven priests bear seven trumpets of rams' horns before the ark of the Lord.' And he said to the people, 'Proceed, and march around the city, and let him who is armed advance before the ark of the Lord" (Joshua 6:2-7).

Notice before they ever marched around the city, God said, **"See! I have given Jericho into your hand."** The victory had not even happened yet. In fact, nothing had happened yet. The rams' horns had not blasted. They hadn't even marched yet. This was a prophetic perspective. You must *see* it before you can *be* it. You must see the victory before you can begin the battle. You must trust God's counsel, even when the current circumstances are completely contrary. You must see your-self as the "father of many nations" before you can become a father to even one child. You must see the vision and pro-phetic promise and know the Lord gave you counsel before you can act in His power. He will counsel you to do what you cannot do in yourself.

They were counseled to walk around the walls of Jericho six days. The priests were to carry the trumpets in front of the ark.

On the seventh day, they were to walk around the wall seven times. Then on the seventh time they were to shout, and the walls of Jericho would come down. Much counsel was given to them, and what an unconventional way to win a battle! He did not counsel them to raise their swords and shields or grab their bows and arrows. Instead, He counseled them to keep walking and keep their mouths shut until the seventh day. Sometimes that is the best advice the Lord can give us—to keep our mouths shut. Why did He counsel them to keep their mouths shut? Because He understands human nature. He knew they would likely have talked themselves out of their victory: "This is no way to win a battle, walking around a city." Sometimes our mental reasoning, thought processes, and conversations can be our biggest hindrances to walking and staying in faith.

They continued walking silently until the seventh day; then the Spirit of might showed up. Only when the Spirit of counsel has been received and obeyed will the Spirit of might show up to tear down walls. This was an act of the Lord—a supernatural display of the Spirit of might. What if Joshua had not received that counsel? Or what if Joshua had become discouraged by day five and said, "Forget this. Forget the promised land. We can't overcome this stronghold. We'll just let Jericho remain fortified." The enemy could have had a foothold. Of course, if they only marched five days, the walls would have remained standing, and the Spirit of might would not have showed up. Or, what if on the seventh day they had only marched around once?

The Spirit of counsel is all about faith and obedience to prophetic counsel received through dreams, visions, words of knowledge, words of wisdom, discernment, prophecy, or revelation. You simply act on that counsel in faith and obedience. Sometimes this is difficult to accept, because we want to feel like we are contributing to anything big that happens. But when it comes to the Spirit of counsel and might, all we can take credit for is receiving counsel and being obedient.

When Moses went up in the mountain to have a face-to-face encounter with the Lord, the Lord gave him counsel. He showed him the heavenly tabernacle, which is also seen in Revelation, then counseled him on the design for the earthly tabernacle. Once He showed him the blueprint for the heavenly tabernacle, He counseled him to build one on earth. But what if Moses had been so moved by the heavenly vision that he never came down from the mountain to build one on earth? What if he said, "Why build an earthly tabernacle when there's a heavenly one?"

Just when we *think* we know all the answers, God changes the questions. This is not because God is elusive, but because He doesn't want us to reach the place where we *think* we have God all figured out. Because when we do have Him figured out, that's not really God. It is only an idol, framework, or image of what we *think* is God—not who God really is. That is why Paul spoke so much about the "mystery of God" and the **"fellowship of the mystery" (see Ephesians 3:9)**. The "fellowship of the mystery" of Christ is a beautiful, ongoing, developing mystery.

"Christ in you, the hope of glory" is a continuous unfolding revelation of Christ that happens when we passionately pursue Him. The "fellowship of the mystery" means there will always be an element of the Lord that intrigues our human minds and remains a mystery until it is fully revealed. Every aspect of God's mystery will eventually be tied together. Revelation 10:7 speaks of a day when the seventh angel will sound, and the mystery of God will be finished or completed.

Just as there are seven Spirits of God, it's not a coincidence the New Testament speaks of seven mysteries. There will come a time when all the pieces of the puzzle will come together, all the dots will be connected, all mysteries will make sense, and we will truly see the complete picture and stand in awe. We will be overcome by the Lord as the mysteries of the ages culminate in one moment. Then, we will truly see the "big picture."

If Moses had not been obedient to build a tabernacle on earth according to the heavenly counsel and blueprint God gave him, we would not have had an Old Testament sacrificial system. And without that, we would not have types and shadows to help us understand what Christ attained and fulfilled for us in His death, burial, and resurrection. Nor would we understand how to approach God, much less how God approaches us. But because Moses *was* obedient to the Spirit of counsel, we can better understand *why* Jesus came. We can also better understand why, when He came, He used different methods to heal each blind person.

On one, He rubbed mud on his eyes; on another, He spat. On yet another, He simply spoke words. On one man, He prayed and laid His hands on him twice. The first time, he saw men as trees. The second time, he was completely healed. In each case, the blindness was unique, so each case of healing was unique. It would be much easier to do "cookie-cutter" healings, saying and doing the same thing each time, and keeping it simple and consistent for the sake of simplicity and consistency.

No, Jesus rubbed mud in one man's eyes, spat in another man's eyes, then asked him to go wash in the pool of Siloam, and just spoke to another. Why was each different? Because Jesus said, **"The son can do nothing of Himself, but what He sees the Father do" (see John 5:19).** Jesus demonstrated the importance of obeying the Spirit of counsel. He did *not* develop a template for how church should be done, or what prophetic ministry should look like based on what was done in the past, or by expecting every situation to be the same. Our God is a creator, and He is creative. The Spirit of counsel involved spit, the pool of Siloam, and telling a blind man to walk hundreds of feet from town to town to find the pool and wash his eyes.

God gives us the Spirit of counsel to test our faith. If the ministry of miracles, the supernatural, and answered prayer was always the same, we would not need the "fellowship of the mystery." We would *think* we had God all figured out, and we would have all ministry boiled down to steps and methods. The Lord is not that easy to figure out. He is mysterious. Yes, we can know Him. Yes, we can continue our pursuit to know Him, but He wants us to remain in the "fellowship of the mystery." He wants us to keep guessing and to keep pursuing Him.

We know Jesus was fully God and fully man—and still is—but if Jesus was only a man, He definitely would have done things differently. He likely would have methodically ministered to the blind. However, since the Spirit of might is predicated on the Spirit of counsel and faith, each unique method of healing was downloaded to Jesus when He went away at night or early in the morning to pray and spend time with the Father, waiting for the Spirit of counsel to show Him what to do. Because Jesus did this, He knew what He would do, what disease He would address, and where He would go each day. That is how He knew to show up at Jacob's well in Samaria at a certain time. All He needed to do was show up and speak, and the Spirit of might and miracles was there. This happened repeatedly throughout Jesus' ministry. He waited for His Father and for the Spirit of counsel. Consequently, Jesus is the best example of what it looks like to partner with the Spirit of counsel and might.

There is no need to force or try to make things happen. Just get in the secret place where you can hear the Spirit's direct commands, and you too will show up at the right place, at the right time, and pray and help the right person, because the Lord showed you beforehand. If you go to this place at this time, someone will be there that is battling with cancer or suicide. All you must do is show up. When they see your smile, when you pray for their breakthrough, the evil spirits will leave them.

Once we receive the Spirit of counsel, all we must do is show up. The Spirit of God does the work. He is simply looking for someone on earth to partner with, who will do what was shown to them from heaven. The Lord taught us to pray in the Lord's Prayer, **"Your will be done on earth as it is in heaven" (see Matthew 6:10).**

The Lord has scrolls of destiny in heaven where our days are written—how we lived, how well our lives have matched up with what He has written in the scrolls, what problems we have had, what we have been involved in, what has hurt us, and what has caused unnecessary drama—all because we did not know what was written in the scrolls or what the Father was doing. Often, we muddle our way through life based on our own interests and desires or what we think is best, but what if we instead only did what we saw the Father do? What if we could be trained prophetically to hear, see, taste, smell, and touch God; to see and hear in the realm of the Spirit?

We see example after example in Scripture where unique ancient methods that addressed sicknesses and diseases were developed because someone received God's counsel through a prophetic word or revelation—whether through an impression, word of knowledge, word of wisdom, dream, or vision. However, just because God used a certain method once doesn't mean He will do it the same way next time, even if the situation is similar. Ephesians 1:11 says, **"In Him also we have obtained an inheritance, being predestined according to the purpose of Him who works all things according to the counsel of His will."** If God works all things according to the counsel of His will, or according to the Spirit of counsel, how much are we working all things according to the Spirit of counsel?

If we did, perhaps our lives would not be in the predicament they are. We must develop a level of fellowship and intimacy with the Lord where we seek Him and wait for His counsel so we can release His power. If you want God to release His power in a certain area of your life, first seek His counsel. Over the years, I have learned the power of God will not come if even I miss His counsel by one inch.

From Jesus' first miracle we know He enjoyed life no matter what was happening around Him. For His first miracles, He did not choose to open blind eyes, deaf ears, or to cleanse lepers. He could have done any of those things to better the human condition. Instead, He chose for His first miracle to turn water into wine. Though that did not better anyone's condition, it did make someone's wedding more enjoyable.

In John 2:5, Mary, the mother of Jesus, said to those at the wedding in Cana, **"Whatever He says to do, do it."** That was key even when Jesus did not want to do anything. **"Jesus said to her, 'Woman, what does your concern have to do with Me? My hour has not yet come'" (John 2:4).** Mary stepped forward as an intermediary connecting two groups together: Jesus and the wedding party. She represented Jesus to the wedding party and represented the wedding party to Jesus. To the wedding party, she basically told them, "I need you to do one thing. We can move Jesus, but only if you are willing to do exactly what He says. If not, your wedding will not be better. But don't worry, He will not lash back at you. We will not placate God, backslide, or quit church; just do whatever He says. We must believe that whatever Jesus asks us to do is for our greater good, even if it doesn't make sense at the moment."

Jesus did all His miracles this way. Sometimes He would go up to the mountain all night to pray. That is how He received counsel from the Lord. That is how He knew where to be and who to pray for. He walked to the pool of Bethesda. Among all who were there was a man who had been lying there sick for thirty-eight years. How did Jesus know which person to go to, or even to show up at the pool? Because the Father knew the hearts of all those people, and He knew this man was ready for a miracle. Jesus received the Spirit of counsel. He did only what He saw His Father do, which is the Spirit of counsel. How do we know this? The key is found later in John 5:19-21: **"The Son can do nothing of Himself, but**

what He sees the Father do; for whatever He does, the Son also does in like manner. For the Father loves the Son, and shows Him all things that He Himself does; and He will show Him greater works than these, that you may marvel. For the Father raises the dead and gives life to them, even so the Son gives life to whom He will." This ought to be our motivation for spending time with the Lord.

The first thing we can take from these verses is, as sons and daughters of God, we can do nothing of ourselves. If Jesus could do nothing of Himself, we cannot. I had to figure that out, and I'm sure some of you have as well. But we *can* do what we see the Father do. Sons and daughters can choose to do in like manner to what they see the Father do, because the Father loves His sons and daughters and shows them all things that He Himself does. Are you a son or a daughter of God? If so, the Father loves you! Because He loves you, He will show you everything He Himself does—not because we profess certain things or go to many conferences but because we are His sons and daughters. Won't you do anything for your children?

We have a promise from the Father that He will show us all things He does, so we can do on earth what He shows us in heaven. This ought to be the most exciting revelation of this entire book. Being a son or a daughter qualifies us to function in the Spirit of counsel, and qualifies us to receive revelation through dreams, visions, trances, words of knowledge, words of wisdom, discernment, and prophecy. Being a son or daughter qualifies us to identify, hear, and learn the voice and counsel of the Lord. Since God loves us, our desire and discipline should be to wait on the Lord and to hear His voice. If we pursue His counsel, He will show us all things and give us His power and might.

John 5:19-21 are key Scriptures I rely on in my own life, and the basis for which the Father shows me all things, because He loves His children and wants to show us all things. If you are saying, "I wish God would show me all things," know it is important to be part of a ministry that teaches and trains people how to hear the voice of God. MorningStar's primary purpose is to train and equip others to identify and interpret God's voice through the many ways God speaks to us because, when we learn to hear God's voice, miracles are easy.

Learn what the Father is doing. Like Moses, learn what God is doing in heaven so you can show up and get in agreement with what God is doing on earth. Believe and expect God to show you all things. Keep that discipline and keep learning all you can to know the voice of God. That's why MorningStar has a School of the Prophets and Advanced Prophetic Conferences. If we can teach people what the voice of God looks like, smells like, tastes like, sounds like, and feels like, we can teach people to happily follow God and live supernaturally. That is also why MorningStar is primarily, but not exclusively, a prophetic ministry.

So much energy has been wasted in the past doing things God was not doing. How many missed and squandered opportunities? How much wasted time, energy, and focus did we place on things God was not doing? Then we wondered why people struggled, burned out, or were charred. They got tired of church, tired of church people, and bored with prayer lines. But once we know God has given us the Spirit of counsel, we can't wait for the next time we pray, because we know God will partner us with the Spirit of might and supernatural things will happen!

Now we have the down payment, the earnest of our inheritance, but soon we will come into the fullness of the sevenfold Holy Spirit. God wants to show us what He is doing. He also wants us to keep pursuing this. Keep pursuing Ephesians 1:11-14: **"In Him also we have obtained an inheritance, being predestined according to the purpose of Him who works all things according to the counsel of His will, that we who first trusted in Christ should be to the praise of his glory. In Him you also trusted, after you heard the word of truth, the gospel of your salvation; in whom also, having believed, you were sealed with the Holy Spirit of promise, who is the guarantee of our inheritance until the redemption of the purchased possession, to the praise of His glory."**

Several translations translate **"the guarantee of our inheritance"** as "the down payment of our inheritance." This means more is coming! It is exciting to know that God has more He wants us to be walking in. We don't have everything figured out. There is a fullness of our inheritance that we can walk in now. What does that look like? Hebrews 4:12-13 gives us a clue: **"For the word of God is living and powerful, and sharper than any two-edged sword, piercing even to the division of soul and spirit, and of joints and marrow, and is a discerner of the thoughts and intents of the heart. And there is no creature hidden from His sight, but all things are naked and open to the eyes of Him to whom we must give account."** When we can achieve this level of discernment, we will be walking in the fullness of our inheritance.

The Spirit of might brings mighty acts of power—miracles, signs, and wonders. In I Kings 18, Elijah confronted four hundred and fifty prophets of Baal in a drought that had continued for several years, and an entire nation turned to God in repentance. This happened after the Spirit of counsel instructed him to build an altar, cut a bull in pieces, lay it on the wood, and pour on the water, but put no fire under it. Then he instructed the prophets of Baal to call on the names of their gods, but there was no fire. Then Elijah, as instructed, called on the name of the Lord, and the Spirit of might showed up. The fire of the Lord fell and consumed the sacrifice.

In Exodus 7, after Moses asked the Lord how he could convince Pharaoh to let God's people go, the Lord instructed him: **"Take your rod and cast it before Pharaoh, and let it become a serpent" (see Exodus 7:9).** God gave Moses counsel before he went before the most powerful man in the world at that time. Then the Spirit of might followed, and his rod became a serpent and even swallowed up the sorcerers' rods. When obeyed, the Spirit of counsel is always followed by the Spirit of might.

What does the Spirit of might look like? There are four Greek words translated "power" or "might" in the New Testament. The first is in Acts 1:8 where Jesus said, **"But you shall receive *power* when the Holy Spirit has come upon you; and you shall be witnesses to me in Jerusalem, Judea and Samaria, and to the end of the earth."** This is the Greek word *dunamis*, which means miraculous power, might, or strength. The second is in James 5:16 where James said, **"the effective fervent prayer of a righteous man *avails* much."** This is the Greek word *ischuo*, which means to have strength or power. The third is in Acts 19:20 where it says, **"the Word of God grew *mightily*."** This is the Greek word *kratos*, which means strength, might, or dominion. The fourth is in Matthew 10:1 where it says Jesus called to Himself the twelve disciples and

"gave them *power* over unclean spirits, to cast them out, and to heal all kinds of sickness and all kinds of disease." This is the Greek word *exousia*, which means power or authority to act.

The Spirit of might is all these combined. It is the force that exists with power. What does the Spirit of counsel and might look like when the Spirit of might shows up? It looks like *exousia*—power over demons, sickness, and disease. It looks like *kratos* when the Word of God prevails, people believe the gospel, and souls come into the kingdom. It looks like *ischuo* when the prayers of righteous people avail much and undo spiritual oppressions and heavy burdens. It looks like *dunamis* when we receive power to be His witnesses in Jerusalem, Judea, Samaria, and to the ends of the earth. The Spirit of might has power to heal, answer prayer, expand the gospel, grow mightily, and make witnesses. That is what the Spirit of counsel and might looks like and can produce. If you pursue His counsel, He will give you His might.

CHAPTER 6

The Spirit of Knowledge and the Fear of the Lord

Now for the last two of the seven Spirits of God. In Isaiah 11:2 where all seven Spirits are mentioned, the Spirit of the Lord is mentioned separately, then the remaining six are coupled together: **"The Spirit of the Lord shall rest upon Him, the Spirit of wisdom and understanding, the Spirit of counsel and might, the Spirit of knowledge and of the fear of the Lord."** God is the Spirit of the Lord, then the Spirit of wisdom and understanding are coupled, the Spirit of counsel and might are coupled, and the Spirit of knowledge and the fear of the Lord are coupled. The latter is the third and last coupling.

The Spirit of knowledge is an endless flow of inspiration, or a continuous flow of the come-and-go spiritual gift of a word of knowledge. Though a word of knowledge can come and go, the Spirit of knowledge is always present. The Spirit of knowledge also allows us to see God as He truly is and enables us to become intimately acquainted with Him through the

Scriptures. When Genesis 4:1 says, **"Now Adam knew Eve his wife, and she conceived,"** that was a different type of intimacy. Yes, we can become vulnerable, open, and transparent before the Lord, but this is a spiritual intimacy. More than just a knowledge of church history, theology, or biblical scholarship (though these are all important), the Spirit of knowledge has to do with spiritual intimacy. It is knowing the Lord, His ways, His thoughts, and His person by the Spirit.

I John 2:20 says, **"But you have an anointing from the Holy One, and you know all things."** This verse is often taken out of context to mean we do not need fivefold ministers, pastors, or teachers. However, this is an erroneous interpretation, since the body of Christ is clearly not yet in a place where we no longer need teachers. Now you might think, "I don't know all things. How can this be true?" But you *do* know all things. Maybe you have not yet tapped into all that experiential knowledge that comes from knowing the Lord.

Prophetic revelation brings a part of this knowledge to us, but the knowledge of all things is also available to us by the Spirit. Any time the Lord wants to reveal something to us, He can, and He will. This knowledge comes to us in our inner man by the Holy Spirit who dwells in us. The more we encounter the Lord and get to know Him, the more the Spirit of knowledge can bring us into the knowledge of God. This is supernatural knowledge. The Spirit of knowledge can teach us without us having to read it or have someone verbally tell us something.

The Spirit of knowledge can also tell us what to say. Like Jesus said when He commissioned His disciples to go preach: **"Do not worry about how or what you should speak. For**

it will be given to you in that hour what you should speak; for it is not you who speak, but the Spirit of your Father who speaks in you" (Matthew 10:19-20). The Holy Spirit or Spirit of knowledge will give you the words to say, teach, impart, and reveal Christ to people. The Spirit of knowledge always supersedes head knowledge, while the experiential knowledge that comes from encounters with God provides the most important revelations. I believe this is where we are heading and where we will soon arrive.

We are not there yet, but there will come a time when Isaiah 54:13 will be fulfilled: **"All your children shall be taught by the Lord, and great shall be the peace of your children."** People will ask, "How did you see that? How did you understand that? How did you learn that? Who taught you that? What book have you been reading, or what teacher have you been following?" And you can answer them with Isaiah 54:13: "All our children are taught by the Lord." Though the Lord is not always readily visible, He is always readily available to us. How will we be taught by the Lord? By knowing Him intimately to where He can teach us all things by the Spirit, things we could not learn verbally or through written texts. It's exciting to know this is coming.

Another important passage that piggybacks on Isaiah 54:13 and speaks to the acceleration or increase of the Spirit of knowledge is Jeremiah 31:33: **"But this is the covenant that I will make with the house of Israel after those days, says the Lord: I will put My law in their minds, and write it on their hearts; and I will be their God, and they shall be My people."** This is interesting because verse 31 says, **"Behold, the days are coming, says the Lord, when I will make a new covenant with the house of Israel and with the house**

of Judah." Then verse 33 says, **"after those days."** After *what* days? Evidently, after the days of the new covenant, a time will come when God writes what could only previously be learned by textbooks, manuals, and written Scriptures on our hearts.

This will be an invitation to know, receive, and learn by the Spirit. This will be both a knowing by the Spirit and a learning about the Spirit. Now, verse 34: **"No more shall every man teach his neighbor, and every man his brother saying, 'Know the Lord,' for they shall all know Me, from the least of them to the greatest of them, says the Lord. For I will forgive their iniquity, and their sin I will remember no more."**

Friends, this is something we have yet to experience. Can you recall a time in history when all people, from the least to the greatest, youngest to oldest, knew the Lord? Yet, that is what this passage says. He said, **"they shall *all* know Me,"** and the best part of this verse is that we will no longer have to teach our neighbors. This speaks of a time in the future when we will have grown up **"in all things into Him who is the head—Christ" (see Ephesians 4:15).** The fivefold ministry of the apostle, prophet, evangelist, pastor, and teacher will have perfected the saints and matured the body **"to the knowledge of the Son of God, to a perfect man; to the measure of the stature of the fullness of Christ" (see Ephesians 4:13).**

All creation is groaning, waiting, and longing for that one new man—that perfect, fully edified, matured body that will reach a place where it no longer needs to teach anyone anymore. The Lord will become so real and so available among us that we will no longer need to teach our neighbors, our brothers, our sisters, or our families. No longer will we say,

"Hey, would you like to know what the Lord did for me? Let me tell you how God has moved in my life." In other words, the word of our testimony will no longer be required. All will know the Lord because the Spirit of knowledge, like the other seven Spirits, will have fully grown and matured the body of Christ to where the Spirit and the bride are one.

That is why the book of Revelation ends with, **"And the Spirit and the bride say, 'Come!'" (see Revelation 22:17)** The voice of the Spirit will become louder, and we will teach, explain, and impart things better than we ever could through our own words or through the fivefold ministry. Today, we still need the fivefold ministry, but there will come a day when the Spirit of knowledge, which is available to us now, can do so much more. The Spirit of knowledge will accomplish far beyond what we ever could through teaching and preaching.

Until then, we need preaching. The Scripture says, it pleased God to use the foolishness of preaching to save those who believe (see I Corinthians 1:21). But one day soon all **"the earth will be filled with the knowledge of the glory of the Lord, as the waters cover the sea" (see Habakkuk 2:14).** When that happens, we will no longer need to say to our neighbor, "Hey, let me tell you about Jesus." No, the Lord will have become so real and so near that the veil between us will be removed, and everyone will know the Lord more than they ever could by reading the Bible, which is now available.

When God reveals Himself in this way, the whole world will have a "Damascus Road" experience—fully realizing who Jesus is. This is what we need more than anything else—the Spirit of knowledge to overtake us. We want to receive this knowledge of the glory of the Lord that will cover the earth because this is the universal outpouring in which all our children, neighbors, and people we have been trying to witness to and disciple will be taught by the Lord Himself. No longer will we need to witness or disciple; the Lord Himself will do it.

I don't even know what that fully looks like. None of us know, but it is coming—an acceleration and advancing of the seven Spirits of God. When people understand and know, for example, that God is a Deliverer, that will become revelation to them, not just information. Every scriptural promise and everything available to us in Scripture will become more than just head knowledge but experiential knowledge.

In other words, the Lord will take us back to the way it was in the beginning. Humanity will once again be faced with the Tree of the Knowledge of Good and Evil, which is pretty much how we operate now, and we are currently limited to this level of living. However, then we will also have a new level of life available to us—the Tree of Life. This level will not involve intellectualism, humanism, indoctrination, teaching, preaching, or fivefold ministry, but the Lord Himself will become near to where the least to the greatest will understand the Lord and His children. He will speak the language of the least just as He will speak the language of the most advanced and educated. That is the Spirit of knowledge.

The Spirit of knowledge can grow in a meditative, contemplative lifestyle to where we can completely detach ourselves from the distractions and social media technology that surround us and spend time with the Lord. We can also quiet the busyness of our minds while posturing ourselves before the Lord. We can say, "All right, Lord. I am waiting on You. Teach me by the Spirit. Show me by the Spirit, visions, revelation, and knowledge." This is done not by might, nor by power, but by the Spirit. This is what we are coming into, and this will happen when we are no longer trying to do it by might or by power, but by His Spirit.

The Spirit of knowledge is amazing! I hope, as you read this, you will receive an impartation of the Spirit of knowledge that goes even beyond what I am saying. This is coming, and it is something we will all grow into. It's exciting to know there is coming a time when the Spirit of knowledge will advance in the earth and the company of believers will consist of the entire earth from the least to the greatest. All will know the Lord, and the Spirit of knowledge will put me out of a job! I will no longer need to preach or teach because the Holy Spirit will become so real, so close, so near, that He Himself will be our Teacher.

Based on my own experience in the church world, the Spirit of the fear of the Lord, the last of the seven Spirits, is also the most neglected. Unfortunately, many theologies have drifted from the Spirit of knowledge and of the fear of the Lord. Without the Spirit of the fear of the Lord, we cannot receive the other seven Spirits. The Spirit of the fear of the Lord is the only one that can guard us from presumption or carelessness, and the only one that can guard us from false and erroneous doctrines and keep us in the reverential fear of God. Perhaps that is why the Spirit of the fear of the Lord is the most neglected, and perhaps why it is also the most important. Without it, gifted people like you and I can become danger-ous and cause more harm than good.

In Isaiah 11:3, still speaking of the Messiah, just after the seven Spirits of God are mentioned, it says, **"His delight is in the fear of the Lord...."** The fear of the Lord guards our hearts and enables us to depart from evil. For example, when we begin to move in the Spirit of might with supernatural signs and wonders, the fear of the Lord can keep us from becoming flippant, arrogant, or careless. The fear of the Lord means to revere God's majesty, holiness, and Spirit of holiness, all of which are mentioned in the Bible.

Exodus 20:18 says, **"Now all the people witnessed the thunderings, the lightning flashes, the sound of the trumpet, and the mountain smoking; and when the people saw it, they trembled and stood far off."** Then verse 20 says, **"And Moses said to the people, 'Do not fear; for God has come to test you, and that His fear may be before you, so that you may not sin.'"** More than anything else, the Spirit of the fear of the Lord will keep our hearts and lives in check. When we are easily drawn away from knowing and walking with the Lord with great reverence, we can not only mislead others, but we can also misrepresent Him. We don't ever want to do that. The Spirit of the fear of the Lord is the last and seventh Spirit of God because it completes us.

In the encounter I shared about the heavenly library, when the back cover of the book on *The Seven Spirits*, which read, "The Spirit of the Fear of the Lord" was torn off, all the other Spirits of God fell out of the book onto the floor. Then the angel standing behind me, whose name was "The Fear of the Lord," said that this represented the church world, which by and large was a powerless church.

Psalm 111:10 says, **"The fear of the Lord is the beginning of wisdom."** It's interesting that in Isaiah 11, outside the Spirit of the Lord, the Spirit of wisdom is mentioned first, and the fear of the Lord is mentioned last. Yet, here in Psalms, **"the**

fear of the Lord is the beginning of wisdom." Isaiah had a good understanding of all seven Spirits.

Then Proverbs 1:7 says, **"The fear of the Lord is the beginning of knowledge, but fools despise wisdom and instruction."** So, the fear of the Lord is directly connected to the Spirit of wisdom *and* the Spirit of knowledge. If people are lacking in the Spirit of knowledge or wisdom, could it be because they have lost the fear of the Lord? Could this be why **"fools despise wisdom and instruction"**?

Proverbs 10:27 says, **"The fear of the Lord prolongs days, but the years of the wicked will be shortened."** Talk about discovering the fountain of youth! The fear of the Lord can lengthen lifespans by keeping us from doing many foolish things which can lead to premature death. Proverbs 14:27 confirms this: **"The fear of the Lord is a fountain of life, to turn one away from the snares of death."**

Proverbs 19:23 says, **"The fear of the Lord leads to life, and he who has it will abide in satisfaction; he will not be visited with evil."** This verse will help you sleep at night. If you are *not* sleeping well or are disturbed at night, ask the Lord to renew the fear of the Lord in your life, because when the fear of the Lord is renewed in you, you will sleep peacefully. You will have no other fear when you fear Him. When you fear the Lord, what else is there to fear?

Isaiah 33:6 says, **"Wisdom and knowledge will be the stability of your times, and the strength of salvation; the fear of the Lord is His treasure."** Another good verse is Proverbs 15:16: **"Better is a little with the fear of the Lord, than great treasure with trouble."** Better to have few material possessions and the fear the Lord than many worldly possessions and no fear of God. He holds our lives in His hands, or as Hebrews 10:31 says, **"It is a fearful thing to fall into the hands of a living God."**

Proverbs 2:5 says, **"Then you will understand the fear of the Lord, and find the knowledge of God."** Could it be, if we put the Spirit of the fear of the Lord first, we will gain understanding and access to the Spirit of knowledge?

Proverbs 8:13 says, **"The fear of the Lord is to hate evil; pride and arrogance and the evil way and the perverse mouth I hate."** Remember Moses said to the people in Exodus 20:20, **"Do not fear; for God has come to test you, and that His fear may be before you, so that you may not sin."**

Finally, Ecclesiastes 12:13-14 states, **"Let us hear the conclusion of the whole matter: fear God and keep His commandments, for this is man's all. For God will bring every work into judgment, including every secret thing, whether good or evil."** For Solomon, the wisest man who ever lived, at the end of Ecclesiastes and after all his experiences, wealth, and women, after all vanity and everything else was stripped away, what mattered most was to "fear God." This was the conclusion of his life: "Fear God and keep His commandments." This was man's chief duty.

Perverted fear is a counterfeit fear of the Lord. Over my life, I have experienced many fears and phobias like the fear of heights, fear of spiders, and particularly fear of snakes. We all experience many fears, but the root of all of them is the fear of death. Jesus came to deliver us from the fear of death by overcoming death through His resurrection.

Acts 5 has one more passage about the fear of the Lord that is profoundly important: **"So great fear came upon all the church and upon all who heard these things. And through the hands of the apostles, many signs and wonders were done among the people. And they were all with one accord in Solomon's Porch. Yet none of the rest dared join them, but the people esteemed them highly. And believers were increasingly added to the Lord, multitudes of both men and women, so that they brought the sick out into the streets and laid them on beds and couches, that at least the shadow of Peter passing by might fall on some of them"** (Acts 5:11-15).

First, notice the fear the Lord is for believers and those who live after the cross. Second, notice what happened after the fear of the Lord came on the church. Many signs and wonders were done, and everyone was in one accord. No one else dared join them, but the world respected and revered the church. Believers were added to the Lord, and the sick were healed. All this happened because great fear came upon all the church. When the church returns to the fear of the Lord, the world will return to fearing the church.

One more time, let's examine this list of what happens when the fear of the Lord is restored to the church:

1) Many signs and wonders were done by the apostles.
2) They were all in unity and one accord.
3) The world feared and respected the church.
4) Believers were increasingly added to the Lord, souls came into the kingdom, and there was a great revival harvest.
5) The sick were healed by the shadow of Peter, one of God's believers.

In other words, after the fear of the Lord came on the church, the supernatural was restored to the church, miracles happened, unity came to the church, the world respected the church, believers were added to the church, a harvest of souls came into the kingdom, and healings and miracles were done by the shadow of Peter, a believer, without even laying hands on them.

Psalm 34:7 says, **"The angel of the Lord encamps all around those who fear Him, and delivers them."** This means supernatural angelic activity is also directly connected to the fear the Lord. Do you want more angelic activity in your life? Fear the Lord. The angel of the Lord encamps around those who fear Him and delivers them. Now Psalm 34:8: **"Oh, taste and see that the Lord is good."** This speaks to all saints who fear the Lord. To those who fear the Lord, there is no lack of supply. The Lord is good.

Imagine all that will happen when the fear of the Lord is restored to the church. Compromise will no longer be a concern because **"the fear the Lord is to hate evil" (see Proverbs 8:13)**. Keeping people humble and making sure people don't get lifted up in pride will also no longer be a concern.

And, since the fear of the Lord *is* to hate evil, we will also no longer need to worry about sin in the church. And we'll no longer need to worry about gossip or backbiting in the church. The perverse mouth will be put away when the fear of the Lord returns. Our saltiness, as described in Matthew 5:13, will return. And because we will hate evil, we will stand against all unrighteousness, arrogance, and every form of evil. We can put away haughty spirits, pride, "holier-than-thou" attitudes, big "I's" and little "you's," even how we speak, which we are all guilty of at times. We'll be able to clean up our speech.

I pray in the name of our Lord Jesus Christ, the Son of God, have mercy on us. Father, I pray for every person reading this, that You will bring us into an acceleration of the sevenfold Spirit of God, that we will not just be filled with the Spirit but that the Spirit will rest on us. I pray that the Spirit will be fully embraced for His purpose and that He is the One training the people of God.

The apostle John addressed three categories of spiritual maturity in his epistle. He said, **"I write to you, little children, because your sins are forgiven."** Further down, he said, **"I write to you, young men, because you have overcome the wicked one."** He also said, **"I write to you, fathers, because you have known Him who is from the beginning" (see I John 2:12-13).** Regardless of our level of maturity, we pray that all our children will be brought to the maturity level of young men, and that all our young men will be brought to the maturity level of fathers, because we have not many fathers (see I Corinthians 4:15).

"Lord, right now, in the body of Christ, there are fathers, young men, and little children. I pray that all levels of maturity in the kingdom would increase in the seven Spirits of God and that we would all be sealed with the fear of the Lord, that every person reading this would supernaturally increase in dreams, visions, signs, wonders, and that the nine gifts of the Spirit would come to full maturity to the seven Spirits of God. Thank You, Holy Spirit, in Jesus Christ's name. Amen."

CHAPTER 7

The Fourfold Face of the Father

"Before the throne there was a sea of glass, like crystal. And in the midst of the throne, and around the throne, there were four living creatures full of eyes in front and in back.

"The first living creature was like a lion, the second living creature was like a calf [ox], the third living creature had a face like a man, and the fourth living creature was like a flying eagle.

"The four living creatures, each having six wings, were full of eyes around and within. And they do not rest day or night, saying: 'Holy, holy, holy, Lord God Almighty, Who was and is and is to come!'" (Revelation 4:6-8)

These four living creatures are often referred to as angelic creatures, and I certainly do not disagree with that. However, the Lord Himself is also often referred to as "the angel of the Lord" in the Old Testament. Therefore, these four living creatures could also be representations, or as theologians call them, Old Testament "manifestations" of the invisible Spirit of God. So, we cannot totally rule these out as angelic beings distinct from God. Notice these four living creatures were within or "in the midst of the throne" of God, and we know God does not share His throne. They were both within and around the throne of God.

So, just as the twenty-four elders were around God's throne and the seven Spirits of God were in front of God's throne, these four living creatures were both within and around God's throne. They are also full of eyes around and within, meaning they have perspective and ability to evaluate their internal state as well as to see in front and behind them. Unlike us, who may have skewed biases or negative feelings about the past, these four faces have 20/20 hindsight and 20/20 foresight.

Thus, these four faces within the throne of God could be God revealing Himself through these four-dimensional natures or faces of four living creatures—the lion, the ox, the man, and the flying eagle. Just as the seven Spirits of God in Isaiah 11:2—the Spirit of the Lord, the Spirit of wisdom and revelation, the Spirit of counsel and might, and the Spirit of knowledge and of the fear of the Lord—are seven expressions of the nature and power of the sevenfold Holy Spirit, these four creatures speak in prophetic allegory of the fourfold nature of God, according to what John saw. In the same way, the Scriptures often portray the Holy Spirit in the form of a dove, and Jesus is depicted as a sacrificial lamb when speaking of His submissive nature in His first coming, then as the Lion of the tribe of Judah, King of the jungle, and King of kings roaring out of Zion in His second coming.

Whether we see the seven Spirits of God primarily active in our own lives, to partner with the Holy Spirit is to partner with wisdom and revelation. What good is revelation without the wisdom to implement it? The Spirit of might is wonderful—healings, miracles, signs, and wonders. Yet I have learned over the years that the Spirit of might does not work apart from the Spirit of counsel; they work in partnership. When Jesus spat and made mud to wipe on the blind man's eyes, that was the Spirit of counsel. The Lord does everything uniquely. Aren't you glad God did not use cookie-cutter methods when He created us? Likewise, how He heals one is not how He heals another. Jesus healed several blind people, and each one was unique.

The Spirit of counsel uniquely counseled Jesus to spit, make mud, and wipe it on a man's eyes. Then the Spirit of counsel instructed Him to have the man go wash in the pool of Siloam. The blind man meandered his way to the pool, still following the Spirit of counsel. Then the Spirit of might showed up and he was healed and received his sight. Similarly, we cannot have the Spirit of knowledge without the Spirit of the fear of the Lord. "Knowledge puffs up" unless it comes by the Spirit of God, because the Spirit of the fear of the Lord keeps us from getting puffed up or arrogant on account of our great knowledge. The same is true with the fourfold face of God. In fact, we will soon discover how the seven Spirits of God overlap with the nature of these four living creatures.

Paul said, **"For since the creation of the world, His invisible attributes are clearly seen, being understood by the things that are made" (see Romans 1:20).** We can understand much about God and His nature and how He relates to and works through us by the seven Spirits of God and by these four faces depicting things that are made—the lion, the ox, the man, and the flying eagle. We can also learn much about ourselves by understanding which of the four faces of God we primarily identify with. This will help us represent Him well. It is not that we exclusively represent one face, one side, or one expression of His nature, but we can find ourselves and our place in the body through these different personalities or gift-ings expressed or manifested in the seven Spirits of God and these four faces.

Friends, there is nothing more powerful and enlightening than beholding the face of the Lord! Do you remember Simon Peter's bold proclamation before the crucifixion? He said to the Lord, **"I will lay down my life for your sake" (see John 13:37).** Do you remember Jesus' response? **"Most assuredly I say to you, the rooster shall not crow till you have denied me three times" (see John 13:38).** In his bold, proud, sometimes obnoxious, assertive, and presumptuous way, Simon Peter basically told the Lord he would follow Him to His death. Yet, while in this state of mind, and while Jesus was in the judgment hall, Peter warmed his hands by the fire with the wrong people.

Be careful who you warm your hands around because they might not have your best interests at heart, and you might be in an atmosphere that is conducive to temptation and com-promise. When they ask you if you know Jesus, they are not asking you because *they* want to know Him. They are asking you because they want to poke holes in *your* relationship with Him. The Scripture says that Simon Peter even cursed at one point when asked about his relationship with Jesus and then denied that he knew Him (see Matthew 26:74). The tide of popular opinion had turned quickly from the time Jesus entered Jerusalem until then. The crowd hailed Him as King shouting, "Hosanna! Blessed is He who comes in the name of the Lord." But now Peter was realizing Jesus was not as popular as He once was, gave into the peer pressure, and denied Him to avoid being arrested and beaten like Jesus—the very thing he had promised the Lord he would do.

Now look at Luke 22:61-62: **"Immediately, while he was still speaking, the rooster crowed. And the Lord turned and looked at Peter. Then Peter remembered the word of the Lord, how He had said to him, 'Before the rooster crows, you will deny Me three times.' So Peter went out and wept bitterly."**

I want you to catch this: **"the Lord turned."** At some point when Jesus was being judged, Peter said, "I don't know Him" for the third time. Then Jesus turned and looked at Peter. Peter remembered his words and the word of the Lord. There's just something about beholding the face of the Lord that brings to our remembrance all that the written Word of God says, all that we said, and all the previous words of prophecy that others have said upon which we now stand. Beholding His face will cause you to remember the word of the Lord and the commitments you have made.

Simon Peter went out and wept bitterly. All it took was one look upon His face. Not a look of condemnation or an "I told you so," but a look of compassion and love. That one look turned Simon Peter from a bold, brash, proud, arrogant, cursing man, to one who wept bitterly remembering his commitments to the Lord. *That* is the power of beholding the face of the Lord.

The Lord is calling His body one more time to **"come boldly to the throne of grace, that we may obtain mercy and find grace to help in time of need"** (see Hebrews 4:16).

He is calling His church to come back to a place where we come before His presence and behold His face again. One glimpse can turn our hearts from where we have fallen off track and get us back on track. Behold His face, and you will be calm. I feel the Holy Spirit on this right now in a unique way. "Lord, let us behold You. Let us see Your face. Show us Your face. Show us Your glory!" Watch what an effect this has on callous, proud, human hearts when we truly behold Him.

The first of the four faces representing the face of God within and around the throne which we will cover is the ox, the burden bearer. When we think of beasts of burden or farming animals, we think of the ox. It carries the responsibility for all and exemplifies this aspect of God's identity. Those who identify with this aspect feel the burden of responsibility to carry others. The ox has strength, endurance, patience, and a sense of partnership.

In days gone by, and in some parts of the world still today, oxen have been used for farming, to plow hard ground in preparation for seedtime and harvest. Oxen are also often yoked together. Yokes are spoken of many times in Scripture, including in the spiritual sense of being yoked together with the Lord. The Scriptures also speak much of breaking yokes that are *not* of the Lord: people we partner with, people we take responsibility for, burdens we become yoked to that no longer serve the Lord's purposes, or just things we hold on to that get a hold of us.

One of the most important Scriptures on fasting found in the Bible is in Isaiah 58. In fact, before your next fast, I encourage you to read Isaiah 58, because it really lays the groundwork and helps frame our hearts for how we should approach fasting and the wonderful results that can be achieved with the Lord when done properly. Isaiah 58:6 is especially good: **"Is this not the fast that I have chosen; to loose the bonds of wickedness, to undo the heavy burdens, to let the oppressed go free, and that you break every yoke?"**

Jesus also spoke of a yoke in Matthew 11:29-30, **"Take my yoke upon you and learn from Me, for I am gentle and lowly in heart, and you will find rest for your souls. For My yoke is easy and My burden is light."** The implication of oxen here becomes immediate in the yoke of the Lord being easy. Through burden bearing, oxen learn obedience and patience. They are not rushed or swayed by onlookers or opinions but keep their pace, ever mindful of their workload, calling, and training. The ox not only represents one of the four faces of God, but it also represents one of the seven Spirits of God in Isaiah 11:2, the Spirit of might, because of its strength and power.

Friends, I believe many of you are already sensing and feeling how this face of God relates to you and wants to reveal this side of His face through you to others. It is so incumbent in this hour that we all yoke ourselves to the ox of God, because when we do, we will learn total obedience and submission. We will learn His pace, but we must remember to never carry this burden alone. The reason oxen are yoked to other oxen is because they **"bear one another's burdens" (see Galatians 6:2).** As we are yoked to Him and bear His burdens—burdens for the lost, burdens for the unsaved, burdens for our families or cities, burdens for our neighborhoods or nation—we must remember that we are never called to carry these burdens alone. He is by our side, as the bigger ox, and we are the smaller ox. When the load becomes too difficult, He will help carry you through to finish the job.

In Bible days, when they wanted to train a young ox to plow fields, they would yoke a large, 2,500-pound ox to a young ox by putting a big yoke around the big ox and a small yoke around the young ox, connected by a plank. Then they would walk the young, unbroken, untrained ox next to the larger, disciplined, strong ox and put the plow behind the larger one. The big ox knew the pace needing to be maintained, while the young ox would often become impatient and try to break free, go its own direction, or at its own pace. However, not being able to do so, it would start kicking its heels or trying to break free from the yoke. Knowing this face of the Lord can break us from mean-spiritedness. God will sometimes allow undesirable circumstances to come into our lives to break us from our tendency to go in our own direction, to go at our own pace, or to do our own thing.

Sometimes the young ox would even sit in rebellion and refuse to walk side-by-side with the other ox. Perhaps you've "been there, done that" in your walk with the Lord. You said, "I quit. I'm done. I'm not doing this anymore!" But when the young ox would sit down, the big ox would just drag the young ox along. Have you ever felt like quitting on the Lord, but then He started carrying you like the young ox?

Other times, the young ox would kick or try to break free. In this case, they would use a goad to break the ox of this tendency. The goad was a plank with little barbs sticking out of it. This would be hung behind the young ox's legs to break the young ox of its stubbornness. Every time the young ox would kick against the goad, its prickly barbs would dig into its legs and cause pain. The more the ox kicked, the more it would hurt, until it became an open wound. Have you ever felt pain in your walk with the Lord? Sometimes the Lord will allow that pain to break us free from our stubbornness, which was often displayed by these untrained, unbroken oxen. Still, the young ox would continue to kick for a time until it figured out it could not break free no matter how much it resisted. Thus, "kicking against the goads" became a lesson in futility.

The first mention of the apostle Paul in Scripture is in Acts 7:58 when a young man named Saul of Tarsus held the coats of the witnesses to the stoning of Stephen. Saul also carried letters in his hand which were basically death sentences for more Christians. Saul actually believed he was doing God a service by persecuting and imprisoning Christians. However, later in Acts 22, Paul recounted the day of his conversion, the day that Saul became Paul, and the day the man who later wrote two-thirds of the New Testament met the Lord, the ox of God, on the road to Damascus.

As he retold the story, he said, **"What shall I do, Lord?" (see Acts 22:10).** By then, Saul must have felt tired of doing things his own way. He was also feeling the pain from the goads, having been blinded by the light. The Scripture says, after being blinded, he and those who were with him were knocked to the ground (see Acts 26:13-14). He had done things his own way long enough, but after asking, what now, Lord? The Lord said, **"Arise and go to Damascus, and there you will be told all things which are appointed for you to do" (see Acts 22:10).**

Then in Acts 26:14, Paul again recounted the story before King Agrippa. He said, **"And when we all had fallen to the ground, I heard a voice speaking to me and saying in the Hebrew language 'Saul, Saul, why are you persecuting Me? It is hard for you to kick against the goads.'"** Here we see the young ox, going his own way, at his own pace, kicking and resisting against the sovereign grace of God. He was struck by a bright light and a voice that spoke to him out of that light. Recognizing all the resistance and internal turmoil he had been feeling, God became the big ox in his life. Paul was kicking and flailing against the bigger ox, but then the Lord showed him: My yoke only becomes easy when you follow My lead.

The Lord said to Saul, **"It is hard for you to kick against the goads,"** alluding to the imagery of the ox and to the young ox being broken. Jesus was alluding to the temptation and desire in Saul to break free and not go in the direction or pace of the larger ox, but God's purposes for Saul were far too important to let him continue going in his own direction at his own pace.

How you ever heard the term "stiff-necked"? You might think of "stiff-necked" as an Old Testament term used for the hardness of Pharoah's heart to let God's people go, or for the Israelites who wandered in the wilderness for forty years instead of possessing the promised land. However, the term is also used for stubborn oxen that refuse the yoke. Even Jesus used this term to refer to the religious, God-fearing, law-abiding Jews of His day who ultimately rejected Him as their Messiah when He spoke of the hardness of men's hearts (see Mark 3:15; 6:52; 8:17). And Stephen called those who resisted the Holy Spirit a **"stiff-necked generation" (see Acts 7:51)**. But in reference to oxen, "stiff-necked" meant the tension that built when these young 500-pound oxen would try and break free or sit and refuse to participate. Of course, this would invariably lead to them being dragged along by the burden bearer to break them of their stubbornness. We often quote this verse: **"Rebellion is as the sin of witchcraft,"** but did you know the next part of that verse says, **"and stubbornness is as iniquity and idolatry" (see I Samuel 15:23).** Stubbornness is right up there with rebellion.

So, that is how young oxen were and are trained to become burden bearers and eventually carry the weight of the larger oxen. As we come to know the Lord better and come into His presence, He will reveal this side of His face to us. He will break us of our stubbornness and insistence on going our own ways and doing our own things. He will walk with us. And when we sit down, kick, resist, and buck against Him—even when we cannot carry ourselves—He will carry us and share our bu rdens until we learn His ways, His pace, His direction, and learn to walk with Him. Then, His yoke will become easy. Then we will know the work of the Ox has been accomplished in our lives. Our burden will become light because He is carrying the load.

Now if you are carrying a load that is too heavy for you, one of two things is happening: either you are resisting His yoke, or you are trying to do it alone. Whatever your calling, whatever you do, *His* yoke is easy, and *His* burden is light.

The next face of God is the eagle, and not *just* the eagle but the flying eagle. We can also see the flying eagle in the seven Spirits of God in the Spirit of wisdom and knowledge. As God turns His face a little more, it begins to take on the appearance of an eagle. We saw His face as an ox, and now as an eagle. The face of the eagle represents the One who is high above the heavens (see Psalm 113:4). It also represents the Liberty Eagle, eyes, and vision. The eagle has a unique ability to see things from great distances which other birds cannot. The eagle is also a nest builder.

When an eagle soars to a certain height, its wing joint will lock in place from that point forward. No longer is it flapping its wings to get somewhere; it is simply letting the wind and current carry it. You may have heard this saying before: "You'll never learn to soar with the eagles, so long as you keep flapping with the chickens." You don't need to exert much energy when you allow the wind and current to carry you. The eagle does not work hard or struggle to soar high; it learns to be carried. Pilots have even reported seeing eagles flying at altitudes of up to 10,000 feet. An eagle can also spot a rat on the ground from a high altitude. They have the "10,000-foot" view. Eagles not only have an amazing view of the ground, but also amazing peripheral views.

It is so easy with everything happening in our daily lives, and with everything we hear on the news or in media, to have only a ground-level or superficial view of things. However, God wants us to have the 10,000-foot view of an eagle. He wants to help us rise above everything that keeps us on the surface, steals our attention, or hinders us from going higher. The old saying, "You can't see the forest for the trees," may apply here. The Lord wants to take all of us to a place where some things no longer capture our attention. He wants to take all of us to a higher perspective.

For example, you may have a vision for your family, but God may be calling you to soar higher and get a vision for your neighborhood, a house church, or a home group. Or, He may be calling you higher to get a vision for your city or state. God is calling some to fly high enough to get a vision for what He wants to do in their nations. God's view is high. **"For as the heavens are higher than the earth, so are My ways higher than your ways, and My thoughts than your**

thoughts" (Isaiah 55:9). God can take us to such heights where we begin to see like Him, where we begin to understand words like, "God so loved the world," not just a city, state, or nation.

When eagles nest, the female will put her nest in the cleft of a rock near the cliff's edge. Of course, we know eagles also represent prophetic people who are also always "on the edge." Mother eagles build their nests on the edge to eventually teach their babies to fly. She builds her nest with thorns for bedding, then puts hard rocks and sharp stones underneath. The thorns stick out like barbs in the nest. Then, she fills the rest of the nest with soft padding made of fluffy down to make her nest warm, cozy, and comfortable before laying her eggs.

When the eagles hatch, they sit comfortably inside the warm nest. Then, when the eagles reach the stage of maturity where they have grown feathers, the mother eagle knows her babies are ready to learn to fly. So, she purposely begins removing the soft padding and comfortable down from the nest, just as the Lord does with us. The Lord knows, when we start showing signs of maturity, it's time for us to fly. There's nothing like the Lord making us uncomfortable after we have remained in the same condition or place (and it may not be a geographical place) for a long time.

Then, when the bedding of the nest is no longer comfortable, the baby eaglets will perch up on the side of the nest—which, remember, is also on the edge of a cliff. They will just sit there and wait for her to come by. Then, when she feels they are ready to take the leap of faith, she will come up behind him and begin to nudge them with her beak until she pushes one of them out of the nest and off the edge of the cliff. The young eagle immediately begins falling, tumbling, turning upside down, and frantically flapping its wings to fly.

Have you ever felt like there were times in your life when God pushed you out of the nest? Then, just when you started falling and were sure God had lost control, like the mother eagle, God swooped down and picked you up and placed you back on the cliff or some other high place.

The mother eagle will sit there just long enough for the eaglet to catch its breath, then start nudging it again. Then it is falling, falling, falling, and just when all seems lost, the mother eagle swoops down to pick up her baby and again carry it on her wings back to the nest. Then, she will move on to the next eaglet. She is teaching her babies to fly, and it's a process. Perhaps some of you have felt that second nudge. The Lord would not allow you to remain comfortable.

I love Exodus 19:4 where the Lord said, **"I bore you on eagles' wings and brought you to Myself."** He was reminding the Israelites of how He had broken the back of stubborn Pharaoh to bring them out of Egypt, how He had parted the Red Sea and led them through on dry ground, and how they had come out on the other side and watched their enemies drown under His mighty hand. He wanted to remind them they did not do this on their own. It was not luck or chance; He bore them on eagles' wings and brought them to Himself.

Then in Deuteronomy 32:10-12, speaking of Jacob and his descendants, the Lord said: **"He encircled him, He instructed him, he kept him as the apple of His eye. As an eagle stirs up its nest, hovers over its young, spreading out** its wings, taking them up, carrying them on its wings, so the Lord alone led him, and there was no foreign god with him." This is the process of learning to fly.

And finally, Isaiah 40:31, **"But those who wait on** [expect, look, hope, or listen for] **the Lord shall renew their strength; they shall mount up with wings like eagles, they shall run and not be weary, they shall walk and not faint."** God says, for those who wait on Me, your spiritual life will reach a point of such strength that you can mount up with wings like eagles, run and not grow weary, and walk and not faint.

God is giving some of you wings. You have feathers. You have evidence of growth. You have come a long way since you hatched, but you haven't quite received your wings yet. Now you can soar and follow the current, leading, direction, breeze, and wind of the Holy Spirit. I believe God is giving some of you wings so you can mount up. Some of you are about to encounter the Lord in a new way. You are about to have heavenly encounters. You are about to know the Lord in a whole new way. You are beginning to see the side of God that is the eagle which stirs up its nest and carries you on wings, so you, too, can mount up with wings as eagles, run and not get weary, and walk and not faint.

If you are feeling weary, feeling like you are about to faint, feeling like you are tired and ready to give up, or just wanting to remain earthbound, God says, "No. I cannot let you remain comfortable in the padding of the nest or on the edge. I want you to fly, and I will fly with you until you learn to fly, and I will carry you if you fall." **"Now unto Him that is able to keep you from falling" (see Jude 1:24 KJV).**

Then there's another face of God that looks like a man. This symbolizes the humanity of God, who came in the form of man, who is Christ Jesus. Jesus Christ is fully God and fully man. He had emotions. He felt empathy. He still feels and understands vulnerability. He can be seen, though related to Him is the image of the invisible God. Hebrews 4:15 tells us about this side of God's face: **"For we do not have a High Priest who cannot sympathize with our weakness, but was in all points tempted as we are, yet without sin."** In Exodus 32:10, we see a part of God's emotions like a man. Here, the Lord is relatable, and we can begin to know Him in this way. He said, **"Now therefore, let Me alone, that My wrath may burn hot against them and I may consume them."**

In Zephaniah 3:17 we read that God rejoices over us with gladness like a man. Some of you need to be reminded that God rejoices over you, over how far you've come, and over how far He will take you. You haven't seen anything yet! **"He will quiet you with His love, He will rejoice over you with singing."**

Not only can God rejoice and be angry, but according to Psalm 2:4, God can also laugh. **"He who sits in the heavens shall laugh."** Then John 11:35 says, **"Jesus wept."** So, we know God can also cry. Isaiah 65:19: **"I will rejoice in Jerusalem, and joy in My people."** In John 15:11, Jesus said, **"These things have I spoken to you, that *My* joy may remain in you."** Song of Solomon 2:8 says, **"Behold, he comes leaping upon the mountains, skipping upon the hills."**

God wants to have a relational connection *with* us, and He likes transparency *from* us. He is not just an ox or an eagle, He is also a man—the God-man, Christ Jesus. He wants to

116

be vulnerable with us. He wants us to talk to Him about our struggles or what's bothering us. He wants us to share our day with Him. We have not a High Priest who cannot be touched by human emotion. He *can* be touched. There is something beautiful about fellowshipping with the Godhead.

The supernatural display of healing the sick happens often, in part, because the Lord wants to better the human condition. God fully became man in the Lord Jesus Christ to fully express Himself through the face of a man. This is the third face in the fourfold face of God. In John 14, Philip said, **"'Lord, show us the Father.' Jesus said to him, 'Have I been with you so long, and yet you have not known Me, Philip? He who has seen Me has seen the Father'"** (see John 14:8-9). When you look into the face of Jesus Christ, you are looking into the face of the God-man, according to Colossians 2:9: **"For in Him dwells all the fullness of the Godhead bodily."**

Friend, if you can see God now, you'll see Jesus when you get to heaven. If you can see God, you will see Jesus. Jesus is the complete human expression of the Godhead. He is relatable, He loves you, and He can be touched. You can still touch the hem of His garment. He cares about your needs, enough to want to know what you are going through. He wants to relate and connect with you. Jesus Christ is the God-man, the face of God, and the full expression of God and humanity. **"If you had known Me, you would have known my Father also; and from now on you know Him and have seen Him"** (John 14:7).

Perhaps you have known the Lord as the ox and are right now in that process. You are feeling the pricks of the goads. He is working on you and training you to partner and to be yoked with Him. Perhaps you have known the Lord as the eagle. You have sought to soar high. You have seen the future. You have seen the secrets of men's hearts. You have seen words of knowledge, words of wisdom, words of prophecy, and you have discerned spirits. You have seen things from the 10,000-foot view, not just on the surface. You have been in the heavens like the eagle. Perhaps you can relate to the Lord as a man. The beauty of the gospel is that God became a man. Perhaps you can relate better to His humanity, and you can connect well with humanity, minister to humanity, and heal broken hearts and bodies. You can relate well to the human side of God's face.

Of course, if you're prophetic, you can relate well to the eagle side of God's face. However, when you're learning to work with and for the Lord and pace yourself, learning sacrifice, strength, endurance, and patience, you can relate well the ox side of God's face. But then, as you get closer to the throne and His face turns a little more, you see the eagle and you start to prophesy. Then, you see God in the humanity of Jesus Christ. Then, just before He turns His face fully away from you, you hear the roar and see the lion—the Lion of the tribe of Judah, the fierce protector and king of the jungle.

Last but certainly not least of the four faces of God is the face of the lion. The face of the lion represents kingship, rulership, lordship, and the establishment of boundaries. This is the aspect of God that releases authority, dominion, and the fear of the presence of Someone who is stronger than you. And here, in the face of the lion, we see a connection to the Spirit of the fear of the Lord. We see another one of the seven Spirits of God in the four faces of God.

I believe we are coming to a place where the Lord can begin to trust us with authority and not just power. Authority to take dominion for the kingdom, authority to take ground for the kingdom without fear of intimidation or the push-back of hell. **"In My name, they will cast out demons" (see Mark 16:17).** That is the lion roaring. The Father is a lion who roars over us, while His breath of life is released, and while the sound of heaven is roaring. Jesus is both the Lamb of God and the Lion of the tribe of Judah. He is loving, but there is another side of Him, which will fully be revealed at His second coming as the lion of the tribe of Judah.

There are only two titles in the Bible which the Lord and Lucifer share. One is "lion," and the other is "morning star." In Revelation 5:5, Jesus is called **"the Lion of the tribe of Judah."** Then in I Peter 5:8, the devil is also referred as a **"roaring lion."**

He is not the real lion, but a counterfeit lion. He is more aligned with the roar and with making noise, but Jesus defeated him at the cross and removed his teeth.

Likewise, in Revelation 22:16, Jesus is described as **"the Bright and Morning Star."** Then, in Revelation 2, Jesus promised, **"He who overcomes, and keeps My works until the end . . . I will give him the morning star" (see Revelation 2:26-28).** That is the reward of the righteous, as it was given to Abraham, **"I am your shield, your exceedingly great reward" (see Genesis 15:1).**

And finally, in Isaiah 14:12, Lucifer is also called the **Morning Star. "How you are fallen from heaven, O Morning Star, son of Dawn! How you are cut down to the ground, you who laid the nations low!" (see Isaiah 14:12 NRSV)** If those are the only two titles that Jesus and Lucifer share in Scripture, then we know those two titles and roles will become most important and significant in these last days. If there is a real and a counterfeit, then we know Satan, as a roaring lion, will try to usurp power and control. However, he has no authority. He can use fear but not authority. He can come disguised as an angel of light, but Jesus still outshines them all!

I can hear the Lord saying right now, *"I am roaring fresh, hot breath from heaven, and a fresh sound over My people. I am protecting and I am establishing My dominion and authority as King and Lord, both at My coming, and I am soon to do it in the earth."*

Discernment will help us know which face God is revealing to and through us in our own unique gifts and callings. This will help us to know which face of God we relate to better. In these four faces, we can take on His image and likeness, just as we were originally created in the image and likeness of God.

What will be the significance of the morning star in these last days? In ancient times, when ships would sail on dark, cold nights, they would look to the heavens and wait for the morning star. This sign appeared in the heavens to remind them that night and darkness would not last forever. In fact, it was a sign that night was almost over, because the morning star would rise just before the sun. Not only was the morning star used for navigational and directional purposes, to let them know *where* they were or if they were lost, but also to know *when* night was over and a new day was about to begin.

May MorningStar Ministries be the ministry in this hour that rises before the second coming of our King—not for ego or pride but to be the voice on the cutting edge of the prophetic to tell the news *before* the news, so people will know how to prepare for what's coming on the earth and not be taken unaware. The morning star always rises just before the new day dawns. May we be that last days' ministry that brings light to the darkness. Thank the Lord for His goodness. Hallelujah!

CHAPTER 8

Heavenly Realities

We have now covered the seven Spirits of God and the four living creatures within and around God's throne as four faces, expressions, or personalities of God—the lion, the ox, the man, and the flying eagle. We have also seen how the seven Spirits of God overlap with those four living creatures. I believe the seven Spirits of God will become even more real and relevant to us within the context and framework of God's throne room, to which we all have access.

There is an interesting connection between God's throne room in heaven and the earthly Holy of Holies in the tabernacle of Moses in Revelation 4:5. In the Old Testament, Moses was taken up into the heavens, where he spent time on the mount of God and received the Ten Commandments. There, he was shown a blueprint in the heavens of God's throne room and was instructed to build on earth what was shown to him on the mountain, just as we are taught in the Lord's Prayer, **"on earth as it is in heaven" (see Matthew 6:10).** Since the fall of man in the garden, God's will has always been to duplicate on earth what is in heaven to get us back to the original heaven and earth, which is the double witness.

When the Lord could not swear by anything greater, He swore by Himself, the God of heaven and the God of earth (see Genesis 24:3; Hebrews 6:13). Heaven and earth were in their original pattern when Eden existed on earth. In a larger context, the earth itself was meant to be a paradise for man, who was made in the image and likeness of God. Man's role was to implement God's rule on earth as it was in heaven (see Genesis 1:26).

The New Testament gospel is also about taking Adam's Genesis 1 mandate to rule and take dominion as God's representatives and ambassadors on the earth, just as God rules in the heavens. Psalm 115:16 says, **"The heaven, even the heavens, are the Lord's; but the earth He has given to the children of men."** So, as you read the Bible, always think of it within the context of a book of restoration. That is why Revelation ends where Genesis begins—with the Tree of Life. In Genesis 2:8-9, God placed man in the garden and gave him access to the Tree of Life. After the fall, in Genesis 3:22-24, that access was removed. Then, in Revelation 22:2, the Tree of Life was restored.

What does all this have to do with the seven Spirits of God? According to Revelation 5:6, the seven Spirits of God were **"sent out into all the earth."** This was to help man recover all that was lost in the garden since the fall. The kingdom age, or age to come, is all about man ruling and reigning on earth with Christ. He has made us a kingdom of priests to rule and to reign with Christ (see Exodus 19:6; Revelation 1:6; 5:10 NLT) and to fulfill Adam's original mandate to rule the earth.

The gospel story is beautiful when you think about it. In the beginning, the first Adam was told, **"but of the tree of**

knowledge of good and evil you shall not eat, for in the day you eat of it you shall surely die" (Genesis 2:17). There were two trees highlighted in the garden, the Tree of Life and the Tree of the Knowledge of Good and Evil. The warning was, if you ate from the Tree of the Knowledge of Good and Evil, you would die. And of course, that's exactly what happened. Adam and Eve partook of the tree and died spiritually as death began to work in them physically as well. They lost access to paradise, to the throne room of God, and to fellowship and intimacy with Him.

The gospel is about restoring all that and more. The first Adam traded the Tree of Life for the tree of death. Jesus, the last Adam, carried the tree of death to restore mankind's access to the Tree of Life. So, Jesus, the last Adam, the captain of our souls and of the new creation of which we all partake, initiated the great reversal of what Adam and Eve initiated in the fall. In fact, much of redemption has been accomplished since that moment in the garden.

God's relationship with man continues throughout the Bible. Of course, we are familiar with Adam and Eve having fellowship with God in the garden in the cool of the day (see Genesis 3:8). But then, in the New Testament, we see Jesus begin the process of restoring man back to fellowship with God, just as it was in the garden. The night before Jesus' crucifixion, He overcame the greatest battle in human history, the battle of the human will: **"Not My will, but Yours be done" (see Luke 22:42).** Interestingly, this happened in another garden called "Gethsemane."

Jesus was also buried in the Garden Tomb. Mary, who was first to see the resurrected Christ, did not recognize Him at first and mistook Him for the gardener of the Garden Tomb (see John 20:15). Jesus was doing what Adam was supposed to have done in the beginning—maintain the garden. So, death entered in a garden through the first Adam, then resurrection power was also manifested in a garden through Jesus, the last Adam, where He first showed Himself alive. So, we see this beautiful gospel story and picture of restoration all happening in gardens.

Something else happened in the Garden Tomb where Jesus had been laid. Mary, not knowing where they had laid Him, sat outside the tomb weeping. Then, when she stooped down into the tomb, she saw two angels in white, one sitting at the head and the other at the feet of the slab where Jesus had lain (see John 20:12). Where else in the Bible do we see a picture of a flat surface with two angels, one at each end? The ark of the covenant and the mercy seat where the high priests sprinkled the blood each year on the Day of Atonement to atone for the sins of Israel and spare them of judgment.

So, here in the Garden Tomb we see the ark of the covenant and the mercy seat where Jesus' body had been laid. No doubt, in the resurrection story, His blood remained on that slab with the two angels, one at His head and one at His feet. This is a perfect picture of the ark of the covenant, which is also a picture of God's throne room, according to the model God gave Moses. The ark of the covenant was in the Holy of Holies, both in the tabernacle and later, in the temple. This represented the throne of God on earth.

The ark of God also contained Aaron's rod that budded, representing the miraculous; manna, representing God's provision; and the Ten Commandments, representing God's law and Word. On top was the mercy seat. Why is it called the "mercy seat"? Because in God's throne room, mercy is needed. Then, on each end of the ark, two angels faced each other. This was the picture or blueprint of God's throne room which Moses saw. Moses was with God on the mountain and was instructed to duplicate on earth what he saw in heaven. The gospel story is a story of duplicating on earth what is in heaven, and the ark of the covenant is a perfect example of this. All along, the Lord has wanted His original creation pattern for earth to become the physical representation of the spiritual, invisible, heavenly realm.

Adam was given dominion and shown the importance of implementing God's rule on earth as it is in heaven. Then, like the two angels facing each other over the mercy seat, we see in Isaiah 6:2-3 another picture of God's throne room in which two seraphim cry to one another, **"Holy, holy, holy is the Lord of hosts; the whole earth is full of His glory!"** This must also have been what Moses saw when he was with God on the mountain. Isaiah said, **"I saw the Lord sitting on a throne, high and lifted up, and the train of His robe filled the temple."** Then the angels cried, **"Holy, holy, holy,"** as if they could see the image of God's glory in one another.

Perhaps that is why Jesus said, **"Where two or three are gathered together in My name, I am there in the midst of them" (see Matthew 18:20).** Notice He said, **"in the midst of them."** Something powerful happens when we come in agreement, face one another, look at one another, and see the image of God in one another, crying, "Holy is the Lord." Though we are all imperfect representations of the original image of God, we are still works in progress. Anyone can see dirt, but not everyone can see gold in the dirt and value below the surface.

What Isaiah saw in his throne room vision in Isaiah 6 was the same thing John saw in his throne room vision in Revelation 6 and the same thing Moses saw on the mountain beginning in Exodus 25. The focal point of worship to God on earth in the Old Testament tabernacle, which later became the temple, was an earthly representation of a heavenly reality. Then, when we get to Revelation 4 and 5 where the seven Spirits of God and the four living creatures are mentioned, John sees the same thing Moses and Isaiah saw. The only difference was, Moses built what he saw.

The tabernacle had an outer courtyard, then a second dimension housed in the Holy Place where the seven golden candlesticks representing the seven Spirits of God resided. According to Revelation 1 and 2, the seven golden candlesticks also represented the seven churches. Also in the Holy Place was the table of showbread representing Christ, who is the living bread come down from heaven. The priests ate from this table while doing service in the inner court.

Also in the inner court was a veil that separated the second dimension of the tabernacle, the Holy Place, from the third dimension of the tabernacle, the Holy of Holies. On the other side of the veil was an altar of incense representing intercession. Only the high priest could go beyond the veil and enter the Holy of Holies, and only once a year. As he walked through the veil, he could smell the sweet incense from the altar. Then, as he entered the Holy of Holies, he could see the ark of the covenant. The Holy of Holies was a type or picture of God's throne room as seen in Isaiah 6 and Revelation 4.

Now let's bring this into context. As we see this incredible picture in Revelation 4 of the seven Spirits of God, the

One who sat on the throne, and the four living creatures in God's throne room, let us remember the earthly Holy of Holies could only be accessed once a year by the high priest. However, this uncreated, heavenly throne room has now been made available to us by the blood of Jesus. **"Blessed are the pure in heart, for they shall see God" (Matthew 5:8).** The power of Jesus' blood cleanses us when we put our faith in Jesus and His work on the cross. Our eyes can be opened just as John's eyes were opened in Revelation and just as Isaiah's eyes were opened in Isaiah 6. We could say Moses and Isaiah had "exceptional throne room access" under the old covenant, especially Moses who saw the ark of the covenant in the heavenly Holy of Holies.

Then, after Jesus was resurrected, we see a picture of the garden being restored back to man. Jesus is the gardener in place of Adam who was originally placed there to maintain the garden of God. Then, in the Garden Tomb, there were two angels, one at the head and one at the foot of the mercy seat where the blood of Jesus remained. Today, our hearts are in that garden. As we go there within ourselves and where the Holy Spirit dwells, we, too, can have fellowship with God. In fact, the Lord has put His garden in us until He can put us back in the garden, where the book of Revelation ends.

Now let's read Revelation 4 beginning at verse 1: **"After these things I looked, and behold, a door standing open in heaven. And the first voice which I heard was like a trumpet speaking with me, saying, 'Come up here, and I will show you things which must take place after this.' Immediately I was in the Spirit; and behold, a throne set in heaven, and One sat on the throne. And He who sat there was like a jasper and a sardius stone in appearance; and there was a**

rainbow around the throne, in appearance like an emerald. Around the throne were twenty-four thrones, and on the thrones I saw twenty-four elders sitting, clothed in white robes; and they had crowns of gold on their heads. And from the throne proceeded lightnings, thunderings, and voices. Seven lamps of fire were burning before the throne, which are the seven Spirits of God. Before the throne there was a sea of glass, like crystal. And in the midst of the throne, and around the throne, were four living creatures full of eyes in front and in back. The first living creature was like a lion, the second living creature like a calf [ox], the third living creature had a face like a man, and the fourth living creature was like a flying eagle. The four living creatures, each having six wings, were full of eyes around and within. And they do not rest day or night, saying: 'Holy, Holy, holy, Lord God Almighty, Who was and is and is to come!'"
(Revelation 4:1-8)

Here we see the throne room of God, the heavenly Holy of Holies from which the earthly one was built. Now, in order for these throne room encounters or heavenly realities to be made available to us, we must believe them. We must believe that what was made available to John in the new covenant, and to Moses and Isaiah in the old covenant, is available to us today by the blood of Jesus—not by our good works or anything we have done.

Let's look carefully at these verses. Envision yourself there with me. Meditate on these verses as they become heavenly realities to you and as you grow in partnership with the seven Spirits of God. You must see these seven Spirits within the context and environment from which they were sent from God's throne room into all the earth. The throne room is what ties these seven Spirits of God and four living creatures together. You must understand this environment and see yourself having access there, otherwise these dots will remain unconnected. This revelation of God's throne room has been made available to you.

John said, **"After these things I looked, and behold, a door standing open in heaven."** First, the Greek word for **"door"** here is *thura*, which means portal, door, gate, or entrance. What John saw was a portal, door, or gate being opened to him to God's throne room and to heavenly realities in the realm of the Spirit. Some of you will find that same portal. And as you find the portal that was opened to John, Moses, and Isaiah, notice that in no place does John mention this portal was closed. That means the portal is still open!

"And the first voice which I heard was like a trumpet speaking with me." The voice of God is often referred to in Scripture as the "trumpet of God" or like the sound of a trumpet. In I Thessalonians 4:16, the **"trumpet of God"** announces the coming of the Lord. The Lord's voice is a clear sound, like a trumpet. It is never ambiguous. Likewise, Paul asserted in I Corinthians 13:1 that spiritual gifts, prophecy, and even speaking in tongues should also be clear, unambiguous sounds.

The invitation was given, **"saying, 'Come up here, and I will show you things which must take place after this.'"** I believe John was being caught up here to the third heaven. This is not the second heaven where angels and demons battle and from where Satan will ultimately be cast down. According to the Old Testament, Lucifer was cast out of the third heaven when he was lifted in pride and said, **"I will exalt my throne**

above the stars of God" (see Isaiah 14:12-15). "Above the stars of God" is the third heaven.

But now, according to Revelation 12:9, he will also be cast out of the second heaven. Revelation records that there will be a war in heaven between Michael the archangel and the dragon and his angels. Then, Satan will be cast out of the second heaven. Thus, during the forty-two months of tribulation, Satan will come down with great wrath because he knows his time is short (see Revelation 12:12). So, before the beginning of time, Satan was cast out of the third heaven. Then, after the days of tribulation come, Satan will be cast out of the second heaven where spiritual warfare takes place.

All devilish and demonic activity will be concentrated on earth, which is why the tribulation will be a time of evil unlike any other in history. But according to Revelation 20, the kingdom age will begin immediately after that, and Satan will finally be bound and cast from the earth. This, of course, will be a time of great peace on earth when the wolf and the lamb will lie down together and children can play with poisonous snakes, according to Old Testament prophecies (see Isaiah 11:6; 65:25). All satanic influence will finally be gone, even from the animal kingdom.

Satan, who elevated himself and was lifted in pride, has since been on a gradual and continual decline through the Bible, through history, and since he was cast out of the third heaven. Soon, he will be cast out of the second heaven to earth. Then, at Christ's second coming, he will be cast from earth to the bottomless pit, which will be a feeding frenzy. His influence will only decrease, while the Lord Jesus Christ's influence will only increase as He returns to earth a second time. Ever since Satan announced that he would exalt himself above the stars of God, the Lord has been diminishing him one heaven and one level at a time.

When this voice speaks to John in Revelation, **"saying, 'Come up here,'"** I believe John, like Paul, was being caught up to the third heaven. Paul spoke of himself in the third person, saying, **"I know a man in Christ about fourteen years ago…such a one was caught up to the third heaven… and heard inexpressible words, which it is not lawful for a man to utter" (II Corinthians 12:2-4).** Paul had access to God's throne room, and John had access. Now, I believe we, too, can have access—and not only have access but spend time there encountering throne room realities, doing so with a level of authority, power, impartation, anointing, and instruction. The more time we can spend there, the more we can bring the atmosphere of God's throne room with us wherever we go. That is what spreading the gospel is all about—bringing heaven's realities to earth.

In verse 2, John said, **"Immediately I was in the Spirit."** Notice it did not take thirty minutes of praise and worship for John to get out of the flesh and into the Spirit. Immediately he was in the Spirit. Then he said, **"and behold, a throne set in heaven."** Notice his eyes were opened; invisible realities became visible. I pray your eyes, the eyes of the pure in heart, will also see God. John saw these invisible realities, and I believe by the time you finish reading this, you will see these invisible realities as well.

"And One sat on the throne. And He who sat there was like a jasper and a sardius stone in appearance." Notice that the most precious stones and crystals that are considered jewels and gems on earth have great value in heaven as well. **"And there was a rainbow around the throne, in appearance like an emerald."** Another precious stone is mentioned here, but notice the rainbow was around the throne. Why is this significant? A rainbow is only half an oval like an arch. When you see a rainbow, you don't see a full circle, you only see an arch or a half circle. In Scripture, rainbows always represent the promises of God. God promised Noah he would never destroy the earth again by flood, so rainbows were set in the heavens as reminders of God's promise. However, notice here in Revelation 4 that John does not see a rainbow in its limited earthly capacity but in a full circle around the throne.

Well, if a half circle or arched rainbow represents the promises of God on earth, what does a full circle rainbow in heaven represent? On earth, **"we know in part and we prophesy in part,"** just like the rainbow, **"but then face to face" (see I Corinthians 13:9-12).** When we come face to face with God in His throne room, the promises of God become full and complete. Here on earth, God's promises are partial and incomplete, like prophecy. However, in heaven, in God's throne room they become full circle and complete.

We see this full circle again in this chapter with the twenty-four elders who are seated around the throne, just as the rainbow is around the throne. Why do we see this circular pattern repeated throughout Revelation and especially in God's throne room? Because, unlike a timeline, which has a beginning and an end, a circle represents eternity; it ends where it begins and has no end. So, eternity and God's throne room are always represented in a circle. God lives in the spiritual realm, which is eternal. The first are last, the last are first, and it ends where it begins. In fact, all of creation reflects the eternal realm. What we see in Revelation 4 we see throughout Scripture and throughout creation.

Think about it. Everything in nature came first from the spiritual realm. Everything we see originated in the spiritual realm. Again, Romans 1:20 says, **"For since the creation of the world His invisible attributes are clearly seen, being understood by the things that are made."** Since everything in the natural realm is a reflection or explanation of the spiritual realm, we can understand spiritual things by things that are made. For example, for a geologist who studies Christ, Jesus is the Rock of Ages and Rock of Gibraltar.

Likewise, we can understand the Holy Spirit by studying water. How many times is the Spirit of God compared to water in Scripture? God said, **"I will pour out of My Spirit on all flesh"** (see Joel 2:28; Acts 2:17). Jesus said, **"He who believes in me, as the Scripture has said, out of his heart will flow rivers of living water. But this He spoke concerning the Spirit, whom those believing in Him would receive"** (see John 7:38-39). Jesus said to the woman at the well, **"But whoever drinks of the water that I shall give him, will never thirst. But the water that I shall give him will become in him a fountain of water springing up into everlasting life"** (John 4:14). So, when we look at water, we see the Holy Spirit, and when we look at the Holy Spirit, we see water.

The same is true of circles. Isaiah 40:22 says, **"It is He who sits above the circle of the earth."** Long before we had instruments of technology to measure the circumference of the earth, long before we could travel in space and catch a glimpse of the earth, and 700 years before Christ, God spoke through His prophet and explained the shape of the earth. It would take science hundreds more years after Christ to explain this. God told us through the prophetic long before science. In time, science will continue to "discover" and confirm many other things which the prophets shared, and which were recorded in the Bible long ago. Likewise, today, prophets can still go beyond the veil and see events in the Holy of Holies and prophesy them long before they come to pass. We can peer into the eternal spiritual realm where things are circular, not measured by time, and have already happened, then prophesy them before they happen on earth.

That is also why Revelation describes Jesus as **"the Lamb slain from the foundation of the world" (see Revelation 13:8).** How can the Lamb be slain before the foundation of the world when He was not even born until 4,000 years after Adam? Because, in the eternal realm, everything is already finished and completed. That is why God created the world with a Savior in mind, then created man in the image of Christ before Christ came, and why all of creation will be restored back to what it was in the beginning. As we see in Revelation 4, through the rainbow and through the twenty-four elders seated around the throne, the eternal realm is a circle.

When Columbus sailed the ocean blue in 1492, many at that time still thought the earth was flat. However, Isaiah knew by the Spirit of God 2,200 years prior—long before science could confirm it—that the earth was round and had been since creation. Since the Creator is eternal, He created something natural, in time, to reflect something that is eternal and not bound by time. So, when you look up and see a circular moon at night or a circular sun by day (don't look too hard), you can know the earth is also circular. In fact, the circular rotations and orbits of these heavenly bodies are how we measure our days, weeks, months, seasons, and years. So, why do we measure time by straight timelines when God clearly measures time in circles? Because man lives in the natural earthly realm, while God lives in the heavenly eternal realm.

The rainbow "around the throne" speaks of the unending promises of God and of God's eternal, unending love. The rainbow is also a spectrum or unity of many colors. Unity in diversity is represented in the rainbow. Of course, in more recent years, the rainbow has been "hijacked" to mean other things which God never intended. "Unity" begins with "u-n-i" (you and I).

On earth we only see half a rainbow, and we see in part and prophesy in part. However, in God's presence is fullness of joy (see Psalm 16:11), and Colossians 2:10 says, **"and you are complete in Him."** Even so, the realms of time and eternity do occasionally intersect and run parallel. As we look through history, we see times when there were great displays of God's power on earth. That is when we see the two realms of time and eternity run parallel. Again, time runs in a straight line, while eternity runs in a circular pattern. Thus, the great moves of God in history have been both circular and eternal as well as straight and linear. When we see these moves of God on earth, the circular eternal meets linear time.

Here is the beautiful part of all this: If you feel you have missed something in life, missed your moment, or missed your healing, since God works in a circle, "what goes around comes around." In other words, what you missed will eventually come back around to you again! The eternal realm is repeatedly found in Scripture in a circular pattern. For example,

Psalm 34:7 says, **"The angel of the Lord encamps all around those who fear Him, and delivers them."**

The strangest military victory in history happened by marching in circles. The walls of Jericho fell after the children of Israel were instructed by the Lord to march in a circle seven days and seven times around the walls of Jericho. What a way to win a battle! Not one sword was raised, not one arrow shot. Their offense was simply to march in a circle. That must have been the most bizarre military strategy in history. Have you ever wondered why the Lord instructed them to march in a circle? It was to invoke the eternal, circular realm of heaven on earth to aid them in battle, to manifest the spiritual in a natural circumstance. In other words, it was to make it "on earth as it is in heaven." On the seventh day and on the seventh circle, they shouted, and the walls of Jericho came tumbling down. By invoking the eternal realm where God lives, they brought God's power to earth and time. Simply by walking in a circle, they were able to replicate on earth the heavenly realm.

"Around the throne were twenty-four thrones, and on the thrones I saw twenty-four elders sitting." Again, notice the twenty-four elders were also seated in a circle around the throne. Then notice they were seated and not standing, kneeling, or lying prostrate before the throne; they were seated. Now compare this to what is said of the Old Testament priests in Hebrews 10:11-12: **"And every priest stands ministering daily and offering repeatedly the same sacrifices, which can never take away sins. But this Man, after He had offered one sacrifice for sins forever, sat down at the right hand of God."** Jesus sat when His work was finished. Unlike the Old Testament priests who stood daily to offer sacrifices because their work was never done, Jesus offered one sacrifice for all and for all eternity, at the cross, then sat down.

So, why were these twenty-four elders *seated* around the throne? Ephesians 2:6 explains: **"And raised us up together, and made us sit together in heavenly places in Christ Jesus."** We are seated with Christ in heavenly places. Seated is a posture of rest. Notice that these twenty-four elders were also seated on thrones. Thrones represent royalty. Again, we also are kings and priests unto our God (see Revelation 1:6; 5:10).

I wonder what would happen if we all started praying and prophesying from our spiritual position in Christ, seated in heavenly places, instead of praying and prophesying from our earthly positions of discouragement and insufficiency. This is why it is so important that we develop our spirit man instead of just our earthly, natural, carnal man. I Corinthians 2:14 says, **"But the natural man does not receive the things of the Spirit of God."** Our spirit man is seated with Christ in heavenly places in victory. When the work is already done, we work *with* God, not for Him.

The work was finished at the cross; therefore, our prayers are more declaration than pleading or begging. We have already been healed of every disease and sickness known to man, and God has already saved the whole world. Though not everyone is walking in the salvation that has already been paid for at the cross and not everyone has received the healing that has already been accomplished, the work is finished. God will never heal another person again. He already has. I Peter 2:24 says, **"Who Himself bore our sins in His own body on the tree, that we, having died to sins, might live for righteousness—by whose**

stripes you were healed." Notice the past tense throughout this verse: "*bore* our sins," "*were* healed."

He has already paid for the sins of the whole world at the cross, but we must personally use our faith to appropriate the salvation and healing which has already been accomplished. We are not trying to get God to save or heal people; we are simply using our faith to transport people from the realm of sin and sickness to the eternal realm where everything has already been finished and accomplished. *That* is when salvation, healing, and the works of God are accomplished on the earth—when we bring that circular, heavenly realm into this flat, earthly realm. Faith manifests the unseen and creates invisible realities, then brings them into this realm, so we can all experience the benefits of the finished work and kingdom of God on earth.

"Around the throne were twenty-four thrones, and on the thrones I saw twenty-four elders sitting, clothed in white robes; and they had crowns of gold on their heads. And from the throne proceeded lightnings, thunderings, and voices. Seven lamps of fire were burning before the throne, which are the seven Spirits of God." The crowns on the heads of the elders represent the crown of life, which means they were also overcomers. The apostle Paul spoke of those who would receive crowns (see II Timothy 4:8). Even today, in the realm of the Spirit, angels and demons recognize spiritual crowns on people's heads or the lack thereof. By this they can recognize authority and levels of authority. It is very important to know that you have a crown, and some have even more than one crown on their head. Crowns are yet one more representation of a spiritual reality.

"Before the throne there was a sea of glass, like crystal. And in the midst of the throne, and around the throne, were four living creatures full of eyes in front and in back.

"The first living creature was like a lion, the second living creature like a calf [ox], the third living creature had a face like a man, and the fourth living creature was like a flying eagle.

"The four living creatures, each having six wings, were full of eyes around and within. And they do not rest day or night, saying: 'Holy, Holy, holy, Lord God Almighty, Who was and is and is to come!'"

Notice each of the four living creatures had six wings. This sounds exactly like what Isaiah saw when he saw the Lord high and lifted up and the train of His robe filled the temple. Then, above that train, he saw seraphim each with six wings. Two wings covered their faces, two covered their feet, and two were used for flying. When Isaiah was in that same throne room which John saw in Revelation 4, one of the seraphim brought him a coal from the altar to touch his lips. He said, **"Woe is me, for I am undone! Because I am a man of unclean lips, and I dwell in the midst of a people of unclean lips; for my eyes have seen the King, the Lord of hosts"** (Isaiah 6:5).

There can be no pride or self-sufficiency when we enter the presence of God or His throne room. When we encounter God's throne room, we will immediately realize there is nothing good we have done. It is only by the blood of Jesus and the fire from the altar that we can be there. Isaiah was given a coal from that fire and altar to clean His lips.

The four living creatures, each with six wings full of eyes around and within, again refers to their spiritual perspectives, seeing in front and behind. And again, remember, **"Blessed are the pure in heart for they shall see God" (Matthew 5:8).** Our level of purity in heart is directly connected to our ability to see in the Spirit.

Next, we will see what activities happen in God's throne room. The four living creatures do not rest day or night, saying, **"Holy, holy, Lord God Almighty, who was and is and is to come!"** This speaks of the past, present, and future: **"Jesus Christ is the same yesterday, today, and forever" (Hebrews 13:8).** Notice this all happens in the throne room where the seven Spirits of God are among the four living creatures and among the One who sits on the throne.

Yet another interesting throne room reality can be found later in Revelation 5 in reference to the scroll or book with the seven seals. And please notice the four living creatures, the twenty-four elders, and the seven Spirits of God are all mentioned here in the throne room again in Revelation 5:

"So I wept much, because no one was found worthy to open and read the scroll, or to look at it.
"But one of the elders said to me, 'Do not weep. Behold, the Lion of the tribe of Judah, the Root of David, has prevailed to open the scroll and to loose its seven seals.'
"And I looked, and behold, in the midst of the throne and of the four living creatures, and in the midst of the elders stood a Lamb as though it had been slain, having seven horns and seven eyes, which are the seven Spirits of God sent out into all of the earth" (Revelation 5:4-6).

Here in Revelation 5 we see many of the same things we saw in Revelation 4: One on the throne, four living creatures, twenty-four elders, and seven Spirits of God. In God's throne room, all these numbers are significant. Notice the **"Lamb as though it had been slain"** has, in fact, died and has now been resurrected. It had seven eyes, which is the number of completion. Here, the law of first mention in the Bible applies: The Lord created the heavens and the earth in six days and rested on the seventh day. Since then, the number "seven" means *complete*. That is why the seven Spirits of God represent the fullness of the sevenfold Holy Spirit.

The Lamb also had seven horns. A horn in Scripture represents power. We see this in the book of Daniel where earthly kings and rulers were represented by "horns" or "a little horn" (see Danicl 7:8; 8:9). Having seven horns represents complete power. The Lamb having seven eyes means complete sight or vision. So, the Lamb, which has seven horns and seven eyes, which had been slain, died, and has been resurrected, is now ready and worthy to open the seventh sealed book. Having complete power and vision also means He is omnipotent and omniscient. Then it says, the seven horns and seven eyes (representing complete power and sight) are the seven Spirits of God sent forth into all the earth.

When the seventh sealed book is opened, which is specifically reserved for the last days, the seven Spirits of God will be sent forth into all the earth with the complete power and vision of the Lamb. After Jesus' resurrection in Matthew 28:18, He said, **"All authority [power] has been given to Me in heaven and on earth."** What will it look like when we walk with the seven Spirits of God in us and upon us? We will have incredible spiritual power and insight.

I believe God is calling all of us to partner with the Holy Spirit, so the sevenfold Holy Spirit can fill us and rest on us. When we fully yield to the sevenfold Holy Spirit, who comes in us and rests on us, our level of prophetic insight and supernatural power will be displayed, and His last days' ministry of greater works will be accomplished.

CHAPTER 9

God's End-Time Temple

"Then I was given a reed like a measuring rod. And the angel stood, saying, 'Rise and measure the temple of God, the altar, and those who worship there.

"But leave out the court which is outside the temple, and do not measure it, for it has been given to the Gentiles. And they will tread the holy city underfoot *for* forty-two months'" (Revelation 11:1-2).

Since the book of Revelation was written around AD 96 and Solomon's Temple was destroyed by the Romans in AD 70, John must have been seeing and speaking of a future temple here. However, even if a future Jewish temple was to be built, God would not put His seal on it, since He now dwells in human temples not made with hands (see Mark 14:58; Acts 7:48; 17:24; II Corinthians 5:1-2; Hebrews 9:11, 24).

The church is now God's temple: **"For you are the temple of the living God. As God has said: 'I will dwell in them and walk among them. I will be their God, and they shall be My people'" (see II Corinthians 6:16**; see also I Corinthians 3:16-17; 6:19). I believe what John saw here was a spiritual temple, a prophetic picture of the church, and the heavenly tabernacle which Moses patterned the earthly tabernacle after: **"And see to it that you make them according to the pattern which was shown you on the mountain" (Exodus 25:40).**

After John ate the book, as he was commanded in Revelation 10:8-11, he was given instructions and the ability to prophesy to the end-time church: **"And he said to me, 'You must prophesy again about many peoples, nations, tongues, and kings.'"** This was also the "gospel of the kingdom" Jesus spoke of in Matthew 24:14: **"And this gospel of the kingdom will be preached in all the world as a witness to all the nations, and then the end will come."** Therefore, John represents the end-time apostolic ministry, which has been commissioned to:

1. Devour the Word and prophesy its message to all nations to usher in the harvest of Revelation 14 and the judgment of the Babylonian systems in Revelation 15-18.

2. Measure the temple, the altar, and the worshippers.

3. Measure the altar, which is the golden altar of incense also mentioned in Revelation 8:3: **"Then another angel, having a golden censer, came and stood at the altar. He was given much incense, that he should offer it with the prayers of all the saints upon the golden altar which was before the throne."**

The altar of incense is the altar of intercession located in front of the veil in the Holy of Holies. This will be a measuring of the end-time prayer and intercession ministry, which will be measured by the divine standard. The measuring reed is to measure the end-time church's prayers and intercession until they come to their full measure in the last days. Then the prayer of Christ in John 17:20-26, **"that they all may be one,"** will be answered. The spirit of prayer and intercession will increase in the church during this time of measuring.

The altar will be measured both corporately and individually, as worship will also be measured both corporately and individually, according to the divine standard. This will be the John 4:24 **"spirit and truth"** kind of worship, which must also measure up to the divine standard, not to man's standards.

This apostolic ministry will be commissioned and authorized to measure the temple, the church, prayer and intercession, and worship by this divine standard until everything and everyone "measures up." John was authorized to do this not only because he represents mature, apostolic ministry but also because he ate the book which contains the end-time prophetic message. He will measure the church and then call in the harvest. Thus:

1. The temple, the church, must measure up to the standard of God's Word.

2. The altar of incense, the prayers of the saints, must measure up to the standard of His Word.

3. The saints, the true worshippers, must also measure up to this divine standard.

"But leave out the court which is outside the temple, and do not measure it, for it has been given to the Gentiles.

And they will tread the holy city underfoot *for* forty-two months" (Revelation 11:2). Here, the outer court is distinguished from the temple. This speaks of those who worship in the outer court who will be left unmeasured because they fail to "measure up" to the divine standard of the measuring reed or rod. In other words, they have not advanced far enough in their spiritual experience, nor have they measured up to the level of priestly service to enter the temple.

A divine standard of measurement is being issued in this hour to gather the saints and to bring them into the full stature of Christ as a company of overcomers. The non-overcomers will be those who remain lukewarm, like the Laodicean Church in Revelation 3:15-16. They will also be those who did not heed Jesus' other warnings to the churches in Revelation chapters 1-3, such as not returning to their first love and not overcoming spiritual blindness or deadness.

To "leave out" here is the Greek word *ekbaino*, which elsewhere is translated "cast out," such as to be "cast into outer darkness," according to Jesus' parables (see Matthew 5:13, 8:12, 22:13). Consider this in contrast to the opening of the "door" to the temple, which was opened to John in Revelation 4:2 and never closed again. *Door* here may also be translated "portal" or "access point."

This is also the "door" to the Holy Place mentioned in Exodus 26:36-37: **"You shall make a screen for the door of the tabernacle, woven of blue, purple, and scarlet thread, and fine woven linen, made by a weaver. And you shall make for the screen five pillars of acacia wood, and overlay them with gold; their hooks shall be gold, and you shall cast five sockets of bronze for them."** This "door" was specifically the "door" or veil to the Holy of Holies. This is the door to which we all want access. So, the outer court had a gate, the Holy Place had a "door," and the Holy of Holies had a veil.

Sadly, most of Christianity never goes beyond the outer court of influence. These are the "thirtyfold" Christians Jesus spoke of in the parable of the sower: **"But he who received seed on the good ground is he who hears the word and understands it, who indeed bears fruit and produces: some a hundredfold, some sixty, some thirty" (Matthew 13:23).** Since "thirtyfold" Christians do not bear much fruit, their influence both inside and outside the kingdom is limited. These are also "Passover-level" Christians. Like the children of Israel, they are grateful to have escaped death and bondage through Jesus' work at the cross, but they stop there at the brazen altar and washing laver. For them, salvation is little more than "fire insurance."

The "sixtyfold" Christians find the door to the Holy Place and to the spiritual realm where the sevenfold Spirit of God brings light to the priests and where they can feed from the table of showbread, which represents Christ. These are also "Pentecost-level" Christians. They have fellowship with Christ and with the sevenfold Spirit of God, but their influence is still limited because they never go beyond the veil to the Holy of Holies, God's throne room. The book of Revelation exhorts us not to remain in the Holy Place but to go beyond the veil. Unfortunately, much of the present church is still in the Holy Place.

Notice the seven golden candlesticks also represent the seven churches in Revelation 2-3, where Jesus was in their midst: **"Then I turned to see the voice that spoke with me.**

And having turned I saw seven golden lampstands, and in the midst of the seven lampstands One like the Son of Man" (see Revelation 1:12-13). Jesus was in the midst of the seven churches.

"Hundredfold" Christians are those who go beyond the veil into the Holy of Holies and into Revelation's end-time temple, God's throne room. They are also called "Feast of Tabernacles" or "tabernacle-level" Christians because they meet with the Lord in the tabernacle. During the Feast of Tabernacles, Jesus said, **"He who believes in Me, as the Scripture has said, out of his heart will flow rivers of living water" (see John 7:37-39),** speaking of the fullness of the sevenfold Holy Spirit.

Notice this also in Revelation 1:4: **"Grace to you and peace from Him who is and who was and who is to come, and from the Seven spirits who are before His throne."** The Holy of Holies, God's throne room, is the place of the supernatural. Sadly, not many Christians go there. Hundredfold Christians are supernatural Christians, and their influence both inside and outside the church is abundant.

As John began to encounter these throne room realities, he experienced the same heavenly throne room that Moses experienced when he was instructed to build its blueprint—the earthly tabernacle. For John, approaching God in His throne room in heaven was like the high priest of the old covenant approaching God in the Holy of Holies to atone for the sins of Israel.

The tabernacle represented man's approach to God and God's approach to man. John was not a high priest in the order of the Levitical priesthood, yet he, like us, was given access to go beyond the torn veil because of the blood of Jesus. All three Synoptic Gospels record that the very moment Jesus died on the cross, the veil of the temple was torn in two from top to bottom (see Matthew 27:51; Mark 15:38; Luke 23:45). The tabernacle, or temple, was the focal point of old covenant worship. However, in the new covenant, Jesus became the first to demonstrate, open, and consecrate a "new and living way" of access for us.

"Therefore, brethren, having boldness to enter the Holiest by the blood of Jesus, by a new and living way which He consecrated for us, through the veil, that is, His flesh, and having a High Priest over the house of God, let us draw near with a true heart in full assurance of faith, having our hearts sprinkled from an evil conscience and our bodies washed with pure water" (Hebrews 10:19-22). As we approach God's throne room, we must think in terms of the tabernacle to get this picture deep down in our spirits, knowing that God is approachable and lives within us!

"I was in the Spirit on the Lord's Day, and I heard behind me a loud voice, as of a trumpet, saying, 'I am the Alpha and the Omega' . . . Then I turned to see the voice that spoke with me. And having turned I saw seven golden lampstands, and in the midst of the seven lampstands One like the Son of man . . . the seven lampstands which you saw are the seven churches" (see Revelation 1:10-13, 20).

As John stood before the throne in Revelation 1, notice he turned and saw the seven golden candlesticks. Where? Behind him. If we study the tabernacle of Moses based on the pattern or blueprint Moses received, we see the seven golden candlesticks were in the Holy Place right in front of the Holy of Holies. The Holy of Holies contained the ark of the covenant, an earthly representation of God's throne.

John stood before the heavenly throne, turned, looked behind Him, and saw the seven golden candlesticks with Jesus in the midst of the seven golden candlesticks, representing the seven churches and seven Spirits of God. John confirmed the earthly tabernacle was an exact replica of the heavenly tabernacle right down to the location of its furnishings. So, when we look at the earthly tabernacle, we also see God's throne room in the heavenly tabernacle.

As we draw near, approach God, and gain access to His throne room in the Holy of Holies, we first come to the brazen altar. We do this by living a life of sacrifice and by presenting our bodies as living sacrifices: **"I beseech you therefore, brethren, by the mercies of God, that you present your bodies as a living sacrifice, holy, acceptable to God, which is your reasonable service" (Romans 12:1).** This includes the sacrifice of praise and worship, the giving of our time, talent, and treasures to the Lord, and daily sacrificing our ambitions and agendas before the Lord. We must live sacrificial lives, carry our crosses daily, and most of all, appropriate the cross of Christ daily to our lives.

Then, as we draw nearer to God and to the Holy Place, we see the washing laver. This represents the sea of glass in Scripture. Here, we can behold ourselves, as in a mirror, with pure transparency, authenticity, and no façades. We can see ourselves as we truly are. Of course, the sea of glass has a double meaning in that it also reflects heaven on earth. Moses saw the sea of glass when he was on the mountain with God and used that pattern to create the washing laver. John saw that same sea of glass in Revelation 4:6: **"Before the throne there was a sea of glass, like crystal. And in the midst of the throne, were four living creatures full of eyes in front and in back."**

In the earthly tabernacle, the washing laver was for the priests to cleanse themselves before entering the Holy Place. They could also see their reflections for who they truly were in the sea of glass. In the heavenly tabernacle, the sea of glass also serves as a floor upon which the victorious ones stand as they sing: **"And I saw something like a sea of glass mingled with fire, and those who have victory over the beast, over his image and over his mark and over the number of his name, standing on the sea of glass, having harps of God. They sing the song of Moses, the servant of God, and the song of the Lamb"** (see Revelation 15:2-3).

Then we enter the Holy Place where the seven Spirits of God are fueled by the oil that gives light to the priests as they feed from the table of showbread, which represents Jesus, the bread from heaven, whom we feed from daily. Because of the sacrifice of His body on the cross, through the veil of His flesh, we now have access to God's throne room.

Finally, in Revelation 4, we see the Holy of Holies in the heavenly end-time tabernacle. The secret to gaining access to God's throne room is to go through these various stations of God's tabernacle in our lives. As you approach God, pray through each station and gain access to the Holy of Holies. In the earthly tabernacle, a priest could not enter the Holy of Holies without first going through the outer and inner court, passing through these various stations, and finally going through the

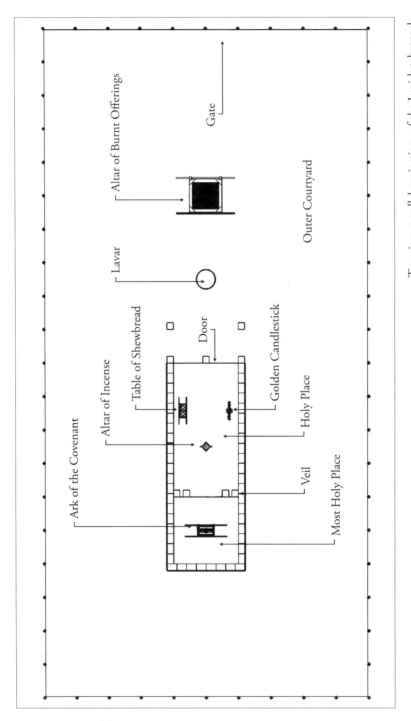

Top view, parallel projection, of the Jewish tabernacle

Gabriel Fink, commons.wikimedia.org/wiki/File:Tabernacle_Schematic.jpg (Label Font Updated)

Sketch of the Jewish tabernacle

veil. Jesus split the veil, through His death on the cross, giving us ultimate, unlimited access to God's throne room.

In your prayer time, pray and visualize your way through the tabernacle so you can process this "new and living way" Jesus consecrated for us. Start each prayer time with the first station of the tabernacle.

1. **The Brazen Altar:** Repentance. Am I a living sacrifice to Him? (see Romans 12:1-2)

2. **The Laver (sea of glass):** Am I transparent and pure? Am I reflecting on earth what is in heaven? Am I being daily cleansed by the "washing of the water by the word"? (see John 15:3; Ephesians 5:26)

3. **The Table of Showbread:** Am I daily feeding on the living Christ, who is the bread from heaven? Has my will been ground fine before God? (see John 6:35, 41, 48, 51)

4. **The Golden Lampstand:** Is my life being illuminated by the light of the sevenfold Holy Spirit, which flows from the oil that fuels each branch? (see Isaiah 6:2; Matthew 5:14; 25:1-13; John 8:12)

5. **The Altar of Incense:** Am I offering a continual sacrifice of prayer, intercession, praise, and thanksgiving to God? (see Psalm 100:4; Romans 8:26-27; I Timothy 2:1; Hebrews 13:15)

6. **The Ark of the Covenant (throne of God):** Am I going regularly beyond the veil to spend time before

the throne of grace to obtain mercy and grace? Am I encountering Him in the Holy of Holies, God's heavenly throne room? (see Hebrews 4:16)

Make this activation a part of your prayer time. Visualize the tabernacle from a quieted spirit as you navigate these throne room realities and partner with the sevenfold Spirit of God before His throne.

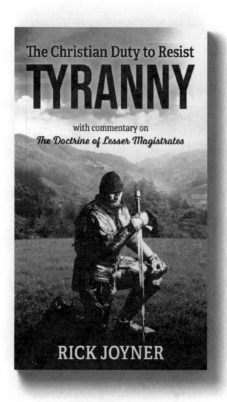